"This book provides very specific examples of what to do when struggling with some of the typical long-term consequences of childhood sexual abuse. I anticipate clients will find this very beneficial."

Eliana Gill, Ph.D.
Author of *Treatment for Adult Survivors of Childhood Abuse*

"Beverly Engel's commitment to helping adults molested as children comes through loud and clear in this excellent recovery guide. I will recommend this book to all my clients who were sexually abused as children and to all those who are close to them."

Joy Davidson, Ph.D.
Author of *The Agony of It All*

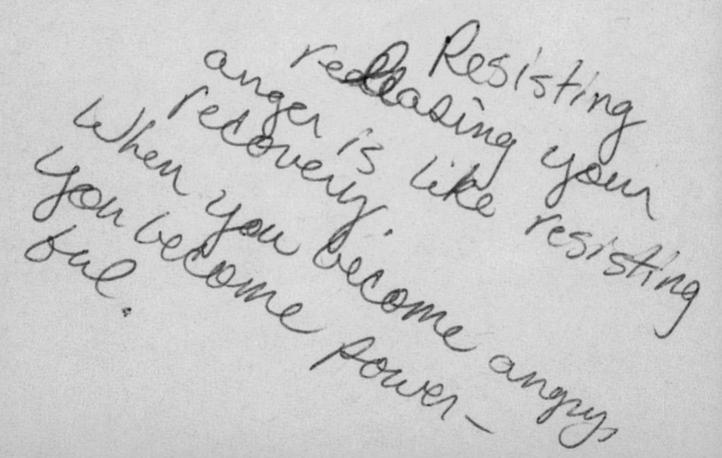

It is *always* appropriate to be angry about being sexually abused. It is never too late to feel the rage.

THE RIGHT TO INNOCENCE

Healing the Trauma of Childhood Sexual Abuse

Beverly Engel, M.F.C.C.

IVY BOOKS • NEW YORK

Ivy Books
Published by Ballantine Books

Library of Congress Catalog Card Number: 88-31972

ISBN 0-8041-0585-5

This edition published by arrangement with Jeremy P. Tarcher, Inc.

Manufactured in the United States of America

First Ballantine Books Edition: March 1990
Sixth Printing: August 1991

This book is dedicated to all my clients (past and present) who were sexually abused as children. Your courage and determination have been a constant inspiration to me.

CONTENTS

FOREWORD

THERE IS ALWAYS evil in the misuse of power. Among adults, it is considered a misuse to force sexual attention upon an unwilling partner. Only where there is equality of power between any two individuals can there be a healthy sexual exchange. Between children and adults, this equality does not exist and cannot exist. When children are the objects of adults who deliberately initiate seductive or forceful submission to the adults' neurotic passions, free choice is not possible. Such children are the victims of sexual abuse.

Because they are forced to accept something that is distasteful or painful to them, these children come to think of themselves as powerless, helpless, and unloved. A wise minister once said, "A half-filled cup cannot runneth over." Children who feel unloved and unprotected are like a half-filled cup. They become incapable of "filling up" because they have come to believe they are unworthy of love. They try to please others, give to others, and care for others in the desperate hope that they may make themselves worthy. Yet no one can give from a deficit. These children have, in reality, become emotionally bankrupt.

Beverly Engel has had intimate knowledge of this bankruptcy. She is a survivor of one of the cruelest kinds of brutality adults can inflict on children, and she has fought her way to an understanding of what it takes to fill the cup of self-love. She makes it clear that the pain and suffering of the sexually molested do not end with childhood.

Unlike many therapists who have settled for being "shrinks," Beverly has taught herself how to become a "grower." In her work, she has constructed a system of treatment by drawing from her own struggle and from her extensive training as a psychotherapist. That system is detailed, understandable, and effective, and involves most of the major therapeutic practices and insights available today for the healing of psychic trauma.

The author encourages survivors to acknowledge their pain and to communicate it to someone who not only can listen empathically but can validate that the pain was real and not a figment of the imagination. She points out ways for victims to discover their own strengths so that they need never be victims again. Although she acknowledges that the building of self-esteem may take time, she offers sound stepping stones to a new and clearer vision of the self.

Beverly also emphasizes that one of the devastating results of self-loathing is the assumption of guilt when one is actually guiltless. She is very clear about the difference between *assumed* guilt and *real* guilt, rightly claiming that no child is responsible for sexual behavior initiated by an adult over which the child has no control. The burden of assumed guilt that molested children carry must be taken from their shoulders; in contrast, the burden of real guilt must be admitted and atoned for by those who did the molesting.

Loving touch is essential to the healthy development of human beings. If we are deprived of it, on the one hand, or if we have been the victims of depraved touch, on the other hand, we suffer deeply. Perhaps the key to healthy touch is whether it reflects the needs of the child rather than the mood of the adult. I have, for example, never seen children come to harm when they received touch they themselves reached for. But I have seen many children harmed by touch that reflected the adult's aggression, fears, or neurotic needs. Most children seem to know when their bodies are being misused rather than soothed or healed.

Children are sexual beings from birth and remain so all through their lives. If we were not sexual, we would be incapable of love or of relating to other human beings. This sexuality needs to be affirmed but not precociously stimulated. Let us remember that the sexual pleasures of infants and small children are pleasures *they* initiate for themselves; for example, they suck their thumbs or explore their own genitals. At a later age, they initiate houseplay with their contemporaries, dramatizing relationships they have observed, or they indulge in "playing doctor." Still later, they attempt more intentional auto-eroticism. In their teens, they begin to feel drawn to sharing sexual feelings with other human beings.

But when this progression is initiated not by the child but by the adult, children are forced into a precocity they can neither enjoy nor handle. The physical pleasure that a few older children do, indeed, sometimes experience is almost always accompanied by guilt, leaving them with feelings of inadequacy.

Nor are children allowed to talk about their confusion, which adds to their sense that all is not right about the sexual acts foisted upon them. As the author notes, such children eventually lose respect for the caretaker (usually a family member) who has lied to them. Worse, they lose self-respect and begin to believe there is something about themselves that is bad. Why else, they reason, would they be treated so painfully and then be required to keep it a secret?

The sexual molestation of children is a double tragedy. It results in untold harm to not only the child molested but to all children deprived of loving touch. Since children spend most of their time outside the home these days, they need all the affection they can get—all the hugs, all the cuddling, all the soothing, all the healing that loving hands can give. Because of the growing awareness of childhood sexual abuse, teachers, day-care workers, and other professional caretakers—most of them conscientious human beings—have become afraid to express such affection for fear their actions will be misunderstood or misinterpreted. This is a terrible loss for the children.

I hope that as readers of *The Right to Innocence* are healed of their own pain, they will give thought to how to prevent sexual aggression of any kind. Parents must learn to give children the love they deserve so that they don't grow up to become the molesters of the future. And all of us, as adults, must be trustworthy models so that children receive clear images of the differences between love and exploitation.

ELEANOR HAMILTON, PH.D.
Founder and Director
Inverness Ridge Counseling Center

Recipient, Outstanding Woman of the Year Award,
Society for the Scientific Study of Sex

Fellow of the American Association
of Marriage and Family Therapists

ACKNOWLEDGMENTS

THIS BOOK HAS been a difficult one to get published. Because of the sensitive nature of the subject, I encountered resistance all along the way. I wish to thank those who were willing to work with me to get this book into the hands of those who need it:

My most heartfelt thanks go to Sharon Kwast, my beloved friend and "editor," who from the beginning offered me her invaluable advice and editing, her constant encouragement and support, and her undaunting faith in me and my work.

A special thanks to Joy Davidson, for the kind of generosity only a true friend can share, for her encouragement and support, and for educating me about the publishing business.

A very special thanks to the women in my current survivors groups: Alice, Angela, Connie, Jean, Jeanne, Kathy, Linda, Marjorie, Roxanne, Shannon, Susan, Susie, Terri, and Veronica. Without their openness, honesty, courage, and determination, this book would not have been written.

To Jeremy Tarcher, who treated me with honesty and respect.

To Ted Mason, for knowing a good thing when he saw it.

To Stephanie Bernstein and Hank Stine, for their fine editing.

To Kate Zentall, the copy editor, for doing such an attentive, skillful job and for devoting a great deal of time and effort to the manuscript.

To Dianne Woo, the production editor, for her professionalism and encouragement.

To Liz Williams, for her belief in this book, her expertise, and her creativity.

To George Hodgkins, for his efforts toward getting this book out to those who need it.

To Sherry Robb, for doing all the things a good agent does.

To Joan Daly, for her excellent cover design.

To Steven Kwast, for generously giving his time to teach me how to use the computer, thus saving me hours and hours of time.

To David Finkelhor, Diana Russell, and Karin Meislman, for their outstanding studies of childhood sexual abuse from which I drew a great deal of knowledge.

INTRODUCTION

IF YOU ARE reading this book because you remember the terrible and frightening experience of being sexually abused as a child, you no longer need to feel alone. According to the figures from the now-famous August 1985 *Los Angeles Times* survey, it is estimated that nearly *38 million adults* were sexually abused as children. Current research, including Hank Giarretto's survey of 250,000 cases referred to the Child Sexual Assault Treatment Program (which appeared in the journal *Child Abuse and Neglect,* vol. 6, no. 3, 1982), indicates that one in every three women and one in every seven men are sexually abused by the time they reach the age of eighteen.

In 1979, sociologist Diana Russell interviewed more than nine hundred randomly chosen San Francisco women and reported her findings in her book *The Secret Trauma.* She found that 38 percent of those questioned, or nearly four women in every ten, were sexually abused before the age of eighteen. In the *Times* survey, 22 percent of those questioned—27 percent of the women and 16 percent of the men—said they had been sexually abused as children. The *Times* study didn't question children, but if the experiences of American children are the same as those of their parents and grandparents, more than eight million girls and five million boys will be sexually abused before they reach their eighteenth birthday.

Ever since the McMartin Pre-School case broke in 1984, there has been a tremendous amount of media coverage on childhood sexual abuse. Numerous magazine and newspaper articles, as well as television and radio shows, have devoted much space and time to the subject. This has encouraged a growing public awareness of the problem and has resulted in record numbers of adults who were molested as children to now seek help.

If you have ever had reason to suspect that you may have been sexually abused, even if you have no explicit memory of it, the chances are very high that you were. It is not something you would *choose* to suspect or "make up." Many of my clients describe having a vague "feeling" that they were abused as children. I believe these "hunches" are correct, because I trust my clients' perceptions, probably far more than they do. In fifteen years of practicing as a psychotherapist, I have never worked with a client who initially suspected she was sexually abused but later discovered she had not been.

If you were sexually abused as a child, you are still suffering from its impact as an adult. Childhood sexual abuse is such an overwhelming, damaging, and humiliating assault on a child's mind, soul, and body that he or she cannot escape emotional damage. The abuse invades every facet of one's existence: It affects self-esteem, relationships with others, sexuality, one's ability to be successful, one's ability to trust others, and physical health. It causes its victims to be self-destructive, overcontrolling, and abusive to others, as well as addiction to alcohol, drugs, and food and attraction to love partners who abuse them physically, verbally, and emotionally. Its victims come to feel ashamed, guilty, powerless, depressed, afraid, and angry.

Whether you actually remember the abuse or not, the damage caused by the abuse only increases with time. This is true for several reasons. First of all, when you are younger you often have many things to occupy your mind—a busy social life, the goal of completing your education and planning a career, a new marriage, starting your own family. Such endeavors are fairly time-consuming and distract you from your feelings. But as time passes, pressure mounts: You must deal with more people, cope with more responsibilities and further problems, and soon the stress grows to the point where something has to give.

As the damage becomes even more noticeable, your life becomes progressively more unmanageable. You begin to realize that time alone cannot heal the wounds, and that a history of sexual abuse is not something you can "learn to live with." On the contrary, as time goes by, the emotional damage takes a heavier toll on you. Pain that has been hidden for years suddenly becomes unbearable. Anger once successfully repressed begins surfacing, causing those who have been abused to become abusive themselves—either to others or to themselves. Feelings of dread suddenly turn into panic attacks, agoraphobia, or paranoia. Chronic depression increases in intensity, causing longer and longer periods of suffering; suicidal thoughts become suicide attempts. Battles with eating and weight control, unresolved since childhood, result in anorexia, bulimia, and obesity. That tendency to drink a little too much has now become a *need* to drink.

REMEMBER AND RELEASE

You can avoid the issue for only so long. Sooner or later, the problems in your life cause you to either face it or go deeper into denial. Most of you will eventually be forced into admitting that it is indeed the sexual abuse that is the root of your problems. Even then, the tendency will be to "forgive and forget," in the belief that by doing so the pain will be assuaged. But a wound this deep does not heal itself. The nagging memories, nightmares, and dark shadows that still lurk in your room at night will not disappear on their own.

Rather than forgive and forget, you will be freed only if you *remember* and *release* both pain and anger. You will need to tell your story, to remember and relive the experience; and you will need to release your anger toward those who have hurt you and confront those dark shadows and villains, once and for all, so they can be banished forever.

The prospect of remembering and releasing may seem to be more than you can handle. As a victim of childhood sexual abuse you have often felt overwhelmed by your emotions. But remember: Your feelings and emotions cannot hurt you; they are simply reactions to and reminders of the devastation you sustained as a child and have *already survived.* Remembering these feelings, reliving the experience, can only serve to relieve their intensity. Even though the effects of childhood sexual abuse are damaging and extremely disruptive to your life, they need not be permanent; there is a way out of these ever-increasing negative cycles. You have already lived through the hardest part; you have already survived the pain, the fear, the betrayal, and the isolation of your childhood. It can only get better from here on.

The key to beginning recovery is to bring your experiences out in the open. This will rob the abuse of its potency. Although the effects of sexual abuse cannot be erased, they can certainly be diminished, and they can be coped with in a healthier way. *There is no cure for childhood sexual abuse, but there is recovery.* For those with the courage to admit past sexual abuse, to talk about the damage, and to work it through, there is hope. And there is help.

The survival and recovery program presented in this book

was developed to help you cope with the devastating effects of sexual abuse and to recover from the paralyzing damage such an experience inflicts. It will take you step by step through the recovery process. While all the steps are important, you are not required to follow each one in succession. Some steps may require months to work through, and you may find yourself working on several at a time; or you may wish to skip a particular step and go back to it later. But keep in mind that you should complete each step before being fully able to handle the next one. Consider reading the book through and then going back and working on each step sequentially, taking as much time as you need.

Over the past ten years this program has helped hundreds of people recover from the damage of childhood sexual abuse. In most cases, individuals experienced remarkable life changes, increased their self-control and self-confidence, learned more positive, effective ways of expressing wants and needs and of taking care of themselves, gained more control over their emotions, and learned to develop nonabusive, nurturing relationships.

Although I have worked with many men who have been sexually abused, the majority of my work has been with women. Because of this focus, most of my examples involve women. But please keep in mind that this book is for *anyone* suffering from sexual abuse. The steps to recovery will be the same for men and women, because the effects of childhood sexual abuse are the same.

SURVIVOR VERSUS VICTIM

Throughout this book you will encounter the words *victim* and *survivor* to refer to those whose right to innocence was violated. While the fact remains that you were a victim of childhood sexual abuse, you are also a survivor. Your tremendous strength and courage have enabled you to survive what could have killed you, made you crazy, or permanently damaged you beyond repair. That none of these things occurred is proof of your determination to survive—a determination that can now be used for healing.

In all my years as a therapist I have never seen equaled the courage and determination I have witnessed from childhood sexual abuse victims. As a survivor of one of the most devastating assaults possible to sustain, you can use that immense courage and go even further. For when you commit to recover from childhood sexual abuse, you also commit to break out of any "victim mentality" you may have developed as a result of the abuse. Suddenly you have the option to be a fully functioning human being, free at last of the burden of pain, fear, anger, and shame that have controlled your life and denied you the joys that trust, love, and intimacy can bring.

MY STORY

When I was three years old, a seventeen-year-old neighborhood boy coerced me and my playmate Joey (approximately my age) into going under a large, umbrellalike bush with him. Once we were in our special "playhouse," he somehow talked us into taking off our clothes. Then he told us he was going to teach us what adults do when they are married. He had me lie down on the ground and then told Joey to get on top of me and thrust the lower part of his body up and down.

Being a normal three-year-old, I couldn't wait to show my mother what I had learned. When I got home, I found her napping, as usual, on top of the covers with no clothes on (this was her practice all during my childhood). I jumped up on her bed and started humping.

From that day on my mother considered me "precocious" and highly sexed. In this way, she was blaming *me* for the abuse. Not understanding that I was only showing her what

I had learned, she saw me as being sexual toward *her.* She did not understand that I had been *sexualized* (introduced to adult sexual behavior before I was intellectually or emotionally equipped to handle it) by the teenage boy and that was the reason for my behavior.

Following my disclosure, my mother tried to do all the right things. She told the teenager's parents about the incident, and he was forbidden to come near us again. She also told Joey's parents what had happened to us and forbade me from playing with him anymore. That was a real blow. Joey was my best friend. Somehow, I thought, I too must have been bad; I too must have been responsible. It all made me very confused. What exactly was proper behavior, and what was not? My mother had always walked around the house naked, and she slept with no clothes on. Often I slept with her. So when the teenage boy had told Joey and me to undress, there seemed nothing wrong with it. But now I had been punished for doing so.

Six years later, when I was nine years old, I was sexually molested by Steve, the husband of my mother's best friend, Ruby. Since my mother and Ruby both worked at night, Steve was the designated baby-sitter. He started by showing me sexually explicit pictures in pornographic magazines as he held me on his lap. I had never known my father or my grandfather, and at no time during my childhood had a man ever taken any special interest in me. Steve was the first. He told me he loved me and that when I grew up we would get married. He told me that when two people love each other they have sex, and he showed me in the magazines what sex was. I didn't like the pictures—they made me sick to my stomach. But I liked Steve to hold me.

Soon Steve started coming into the bathroom while I was taking a bath—to help me wash, he said. I had already begun to develop breasts, and Steve told me they were beautiful and started touching them. I didn't like the touching, but I liked him telling me how pretty my breasts were. My mother had never told me that anything about me was pretty.

One night Steve lay down beside me and put my hand on his penis. I couldn't breathe. Part of me "spaced out," went somewhere else. I later learned that such dissociation—the separation or split from the wholeness of an experience, a kind of emotional anesthesia—is quite common under such circumstances.

After this incident Steve was very nice to me. He made me ice cream sodas and introduced me to all his friends as his niece. He acted like he was proud of me. No one had ever been proud of me before.

From then on I let Steve do anything he wanted. He started taking me to bed as soon as my mother and Ruby left for work. He was a very large man and would lie on top of me and move up and down until I thought I was going to suffocate. I don't think he ever penetrated me, but I'm not sure. By dissociating, I could numb my body and take my mind elsewhere and so endure the abuse. When he was done, he would make me an ice cream soda. It settled the nausea brought on by his ejaculating into my mouth. He would remind me that we were going to get married when I grew up, but by then I didn't want to anymore. If this was what marriage was like, I wanted nothing to do with it. When Steve began to sense my lack of enthusiasm, he threatened to kill me if I told anyone about what he was doing. I believed him; I knew he had been in a mental hospital for beating up his ex-wife. Throughout this time, my mother and Ruby seemed oblivious to what was going on. Because of my mother's lack of concern, I became confused as to whether it was wrong or not. I had gained weight, and a rash had spread over my legs. I also had fainting spells at school and had developed a serious bladder infection. I felt ugly, bad, and dirty inside.

It wasn't until we moved away and Steve stopped babysitting me that I was finally able to tell my mother about what he had done to me. She thought I was lying until I told her enough details for her to believe me. She then told Ruby, who insisted it was impossible because Steve was impotent. Like many people, she thought of childhood sexual abuse only as intercourse. She didn't realize that sexual abuse encompasses a whole variety of sexual behaviors: an adult showing a child pornographic material, exposing his or her genitals to a child, masturbating in front of a child, making a child perform oral sex on the adult—some of the things Steve did to me. For my mother and Ruby, without actual penetration, it was no big deal.

On several occasions during my high school years, my mother would get sloppy drunk and would get very sentimental. Sometimes she would plant a big "wet" kiss on my mouth. Now I have reason to believe my mother was unconsciously being sexually seductive. If she had been my father, it would have come across far more overtly. I had always felt queasy about the way she would look at me at times while I was undressing. Since children do not normally associate sexuality and sexual advances with their mothers, it was not until very recently that I came to terms with my mother's behavior and saw it for what it really was—sexual abuse.

For many reasons, my mother was a prime candidate to be an incestuous parent. I suspected that she had been sexually abused as a child and had in turn "passed on" the abuse to me, which often happens in families with a history of abuse. She was incapable of having an adult sexual relationship, had no other sexual releases, was extremely needy, and had a tremendous amount of anger. She was also from an alcoholic family and was an alcoholic herself. Equally telling, my mother did not establish appropriate boundaries. As is typical in incestuous families, there was no privacy in the house. My mother would walk into the bathroom when I was showering or using the toilet. This behavior was particularly confusing to me because in every other way she appeared prudish and Victorian. It was as if she were two mothers, a straitlaced one for the outside world to see, and a loose, inappropriate one at home. Her inappropriate behavior and leering looks left me feeling unsafe with her—just as my clients describe how they have felt when their fathers or stepfathers have looked at them sexually or suggestively.

As a result, I, too, suffered from many of the long-term effects of childhood sexual abuse. I had both a fascination with and hatred toward men. Like many victims, I became sexually promiscuous, using men for sex and allowing them to use me. Unable to trust them, I was so afraid they would hurt or abandon me that I hurt them first. However, despite my heightened sexual activity, I did not have orgasms. And from the age of nine, when Steve's abuse began, I entered into a continuing battle to manage my weight. Initially, gaining weight was a way to make myself less attractive to men and thus protect me from further abuse. Those extra pounds also acted as a cushion and buffer from the tremendous pain I had sustained as a child. I began to drink when I was in high school to escape my problems and to find the exhilaration and power I could get no other way. I was unable to maintain a long-term relationship, choosing partners who were unavailable, married, or unable to commit, or who were as damaged, immature, and incapable of intimacy as I.

I excelled academically and professionally. But as with other sexually abused victims, excelling in these areas was also a way of compensating for and coping with the sexual abuse. I "lost myself" in schoolwork, and later on by helping others as a therapist. It turned out to be chillingly similiar to my compulsion to "lose myself" in alcohol. Many childhood sexual abuse victims go to extremes and lose themselves in serving others as a way of avoiding their pain. It is no coincidence that they often become doctors, nurses, teachers, social workers, and psychotherapists—helpers, caretakers, and often "rescuers."

My specific interest in becoming a therapist had its roots in my frustration in finding adequate help for myself. At the time I first sought help, twenty years ago, little attention was paid to childhood sexual abuse, and very little research had been done on the subject. After I threatened to kill myself at sixteen, the therapist whom a YWCA director referred me to listened to my story and then told me that I would grow out of it. I left home at seventeen, at which time I began to search in earnest for someone who could offer me some professional guidance. Not one of the therapists I encountered considered my experiences with sexual abuse to be particularly significant.

So I started seeking my own answers. In an attempt to better understand my own sexuality, I began training as a sex therapist. Can you imagine an *unrecovered* sexual-abuse victim spending her days working with those who suffer from sexual dysfunction! There I was, discussing and teaching others about their sexuality while being completely out of touch with the toll it was taking on me. But something positive did come out of this experience. I discovered that many of the people I was working with had themselves been sexually abused as children and that this trauma had caused the sexual dysfunctions they were suffering from.

During one of my internships in graduate school I volunteered to serve as leader of a group of men on probation for sex offenses. To say that I was still in denial and out of touch with my own feelings would be an understatement. I was the only female in a room full of exhibitionists, voyeurs, child molesters, and rapists, *and I felt fine.* I wasn't even aware of how afraid, hurt, and angry I really was. But I did learn more about myself and about sex offenders from that experience.

After graduate school, I worked as head counselor and assistant director of a shelter for battered women. I discovered that many of the women there had been sexually abused.

While working with the battered women, I encountered and worked with their abusive husbands as well and learned that they, too, had often been sexual-abuse victims.

It all started coming together. It became clear to me that children who are sexually abused grow up with a myriad of problems: sexual dysfunction, a tendency to become sexual violators themselves, and involvement in abusive relationships, either as the one being abused or the one performing the abuse.

By this time, research about childhood sexual abuse had begun to appear, and I read everything I could get my hands on. The recovery program that I eventually developed, however, evolved more from the direct testimony of hundreds of victims rather than from any formal research published in journals. I learned how to help these victims by listening to *them*—to their anger, fear, guilt, pain, self-loathing, and finally to their feelings about their parents. It soon became evident that those victims who eventually began to know recovery and healing went through distinct stages in their recovery process: facing the truth, releasing their anger, confronting their childhood family and the perpetrator, resolving their relationships, self-discovery, self-care, self-forgiveness, and, finally, recovery. Out of this realization—along with what I had learned from my research, my reading, and my own personal therapy—came my program for adults who had been sexually abused as children.

One more step remained to be taken, however: I needed to heal my own wounds first. But the therapist I had been seeing, good as she was, did not specialize in sexual abuse. Nor were there any sexual-abuse groups in those days. Clearly, I was on my own.

So I started following the recovery program I myself had formulated. I joined a bio-energetics group where I learned how to safely release the pent-up emotions that began to surface. And, by working through the seven steps, I was ultimately able to alleviate most of my symptoms. Through it all, I was blessed with the loving support of a dear friend. Although my recovery continues, it has taken the form of growth and improvement. My program worked! Finally, I was ready to begin.

PART I

The Truth of Your Innocence

CHAPTER 1

You Are Not Alone

"I DON'T KNOW why it's bothering me now. I haven't even thought about it for years. Sometimes I even wonder if it really happened. I'm an adult with my own family. Why am I having these nightmares *now?*"

Melinda sat very still on a couch in my office, nervously playing with a tassel on her purse, her large brown eyes gazing at me imploringly. I recognized both the look and the unspoken words: *Can I trust you? Is there really help available? Please help me; I can't stand it any longer.*

Hundreds of victims of childhood sexual abuse have looked at me in the same desperate way. Nothing else they had tried helped free them from the emotional and psychic pain they continued to suffer in their adult lives. In Melinda's case, she had tried to block the sexual abuse out of her mind, and this had seemed to help for a while. Melinda had married her high-school sweetheart and had started a family right away. By keeping busy with her husband and three children, Melinda left herself little time to think about the sexual abuse that had blighted her childhood. But lately Melinda had been having frightening nightmares, and she was unable to have sex with her husband due to terrible pain in her vagina.

Her physician advised her that she was suffering from stress. But mild tranquilizers and "lots of rest" did little to alleviate the problem. Next, Melinda sought marital counseling to address her growing sexual difficulties with her husband. But when Melinda mentioned her history, the counselor referred her to me, since I specialize in working with adults who were sexually abused as children.

Melinda had often wondered if her sexual problems with her husband might stem from when she was ten years old and her stepfather began a brutal two-year reign of rape and abuse. As with many victims of childhood sexual abuse, Melinda did not want to admit that this could be the cause of her current problems. When I mentioned the possibility that she was still suffering from damage caused by the abuse, she protested: "I don't want to have to go back and remember. I haven't seen my stepfather for fifteen years, and I don't intend to see him ever again. It makes me furious that it should bother me so much still."

But even as her words protested *I don't want to have to deal with this,* her eyes countered with *Please help me work through this pain once and for all.* I was accustomed to receiving these conflicting messages from sex-abuse victims. Though they often wish to forget the abuse, they also know that they are going to have to face it before their lives will get any better. Melinda decided to continue therapy, even though she was afraid of what she would have to endure. She soon realized that her only hope was in working through the childhood sexual abuse, not in avoiding it.

There was hope for Melinda, just as there was hope for the hundreds of others, many of whose stories contributed to this book. There is hope for the thousands of people across the country who are beginning to admit that they were sexually abused and are still suffering from the damage brought on by it. And, there is hope for you, as well.

The hope lies in admitting to yourself what you suspect to be true—that you have been emotionally damaged by the sexual abuse and still suffer from its devastation today. Like Melinda, you may be afraid of facing the pain all over again. You may even be afraid you will go crazy if you start opening up old wounds. But the truth is, the longer you put it off, the worse it will get. *Dealing with sexual abuse is not a luxury; it's a necessity.* And while the process of confronting and dealing with this issue is painful, it is less painful than ignoring it. Not one person I have known who has chosen to work through his or her sexual abuse has regretted that decision.

In some ways, Melinda was one of the lucky ones; she knew she had been abused. For others, the childhood abuse experience was so overwhelming that it was pretty effectively blocked out, leaving them later to only suspect and wonder if indeed the molestation ever occurred. Still others psychologically minimize the damage suffered, convincing themselves that they have outgrown it or moved past it.

In my experience, victims of childhood sexual abuse start their process of recovery at different stages of awareness. You probably fall into one of these five categories:

1. Those who have no conscious memory of the abuse and who deny their symptoms.
2. Those who don't remember but are aware of the symptoms and therefore *suspect* they may have been abused.
3. Those who don't know they are victims because they don't realize that what happened to them was in fact sexual abuse.
4. Those who know they were sexually abused but make no connection between their symptoms and the sexual abuse they suffered.
5. Those who know they were sexually abused and are

aware that their symptoms are caused by the sexual abuse.

Many victims of childhood sexual abuse have entirely repressed the horrifying memory of the abuse. But not remembering doesn't protect you from being affected. Your symptoms may tell the story for you.

Donna came into therapy because she was waking up at the same time every night and couldn't fall back asleep. Sleep deprivation was affecting her work and her relationship with her boyfriend. After two full years of therapy, she remembered she had been sexually abused. Her awakening every night corresponded to the exact same time her father used to come into her room and molest her when she was a child.

Eventually, the memories do emerge. "Out of the blue," something triggers a vague memory, a faint feeling, a glimpse of a picture. In that one moment, a seemingly "normal" life is permanently changed, with the inescapable realization that rape or molestation was part of childhood.

Many victims of sexual abuse don't know they are victims, because they don't realize that what happened to them was in fact sexual abuse. Some are still under the misconception that they weren't sexually abused unless they were actually penetrated or forced. In addition, many people do not realize that brother-sister incest or sex with an older child can be considered sexual abuse.

Anita was certain that her father had also molested her younger sister, Jody, but each time she brought it up, Jody would deny it. Finally, Jody agreed to come to therapy with her. To encourage Jody to open up, Anita told her in detail how their father had begun molesting Anita at age three. He would play a "game" while he was bathing her, pretending his finger was a "train" and her vagina was a "tunnel." Jody became more and more uncomfortable as Anita related that their father would also watch Anita from a hole in the bathroom door and would "massage" her every night, touching her vulva, buttocks, and, when she began to develop, her breasts.

Anita then asked Jody directly, "Did Dad ever do any of these things to you?" Jody looked away from Anita and me. After a long silence, she said in a childlike voice, "I didn't know those things were sexual abuse. I thought all dads did things like that to their daughters. I thought sexual abuse meant they had sex with you—you know, like intercourse or oral sex or something. Dad never did those things, so I didn't think he had molested me."

Although Jody had not been aware that she had been sexually abused, she nevertheless suffered from many of the same symptoms those victims experience: low self-esteem, difficulty trusting others, and an inability to tolerate her husband's affectionate touches. She could have intercourse and oral sex (those "things" her father had *not* done to her) with her husband but never felt comfortable with any type of foreplay, caressing, or massage. Now, after hearing Anita's story, she knew why. During that therapy session, the pent-up memories began flooding back to Jody, and although the experience was painful, she felt tremendously relieved.

Others may be aware of their symptoms and remember the abuse but do not connect the two. After all, how could something that occurred when they were *that young* affect them now? Besides, maybe it wasn't really all *that bad.* These victims blame their current problems on everything *but* the sexual abuse.

On the other hand, many victims are all too painfully aware of both the emotional damage and its original causes. They are tormented by nightmares, memories, and flashbacks. They can't stop *remembering:* they cannot bathe without remembering; they cannot make love without remembering; they cannot see a naked body without remembering; they cannot be touched without remembering. Like victims of catastrophic events, they may suffer from sudden flashbacks that disrupt their lives and catapult them back to the abusive situation. Remembering as they do, having their lives disrupted so, they feel isolated and different. They fear they may be going crazy. Many of those who have never forgotten have always known they needed help. But they may also despair that there is no hope, that there is nowhere to turn.

These victims may have tried to talk to their families, but to no avail. Most victims find that their families refuse to admit the abuse actually happened, or else they minimize the damage it caused. For this reason, victims seldom receive support from their families and often inspire just the opposite—anger, resentment, and denial. They are told to forgive and forget, and when they find this impossible to do, they are seen as stubborn and vindictive. They feel guilty for not being able to "go on with their lives"; for continuing to feel angry; or for even saying that they have been affected by the abuse at all.

Some of these victims have tried to seek professional help, only to have their problem compounded. Some have stumbled upon the rare therapist who revictimized them by having sex with them. Others have found well-meaning therapists not specially trained to work with victims of childhood sexual abuse who have perpetuated the minimizing behavior of the family by encouraging victims to "forgive and forget." Still others have gotten "help" from professionals who even insinuated that perhaps the victims were the ones who did the seducing, or that perhaps they really enjoyed it. The damage that some untrained, biased therapists have had on clients is enormous. It is no small wonder that many victims stop seeking professional help altogether.

Due to the new public awareness about the sexual abuse of children, more and more people are learning the warning signs and symptoms of childhood sexual abuse. This causes some people to recognize their own symptoms and to look at the possibility that they were sexually abused. You may be one of those people.

Whether you bought this book knowing full well that you were sexually abused, because you *suspect* you were, or because someone recommended the book to you (perhaps your therapist), there is something very important to remember: All victims of childhood sexual abuse go in and out of denial. One minute they may be able to admit to themselves that they indeed were sexually abused, and the next minute they completely deny that it could have happened to them. At any given time they may break through their denial and admit to themselves how very horrible the abuse was, only to revert back to minimizing the abuse, convincing themselves that it wasn't that bad after all. For this reason, I wrote the next section for all readers, whether you are certain you were abused or not, in the hope of breaking through any denial that may surface while you read the book.

HOW DO I KNOW IF I WAS SEXUALLY ABUSED AS A CHILD?

Over the years, many people have come to me suspecting they were victims of sexual abuse: "I have some vague feelings that could be memories, but what if I am just making it up?" I tell them, "If you have any suspicion at all, if you have any memory, no matter how vague, it probably really happened. It is far more likely," I continue, "that you are blocking the memories, *denying* it happened."

If the person who abused you was related to you in any way (a parent, uncle, aunt, grandparent, cousin, sibling), that abuse is considered *incest.* Even if the person was not related to you by blood but assumed the role of a parent to you, it can also be considered incest. This includes stepparents, adopted or foster parents, "play uncles," or any other caretaker who was a parental figure to you.

If the person who became sexual with you was even a few years older than you (an older brother or sister) or held a position of power or authority over you (a doctor, baby-sitter, camp counselor, teacher), it is considered to be sexual molestation and constitutes sexual abuse.

The person who abused you is referred to by many names: the abuser, the aggressor, the initiator, or the perpetrator. He or she used position, power, age, and experience to persuade, coax, bribe, or threaten you into doing something you were not old enough or emotionally mature enough to cope with. No matter how much you "liked it" or didn't try to stop it, you were not responsible for the sexual abuse. Because you were too young or immature to make that kind of decision for yourself, the adult was the responsible party. *It was not your fault.* You did not relinquish your innocence; it was taken from you.

Just because you were not physically forced into the sexual abuse doesn't mean you wanted it to happen. The perpetrator may have played on your trust to coerce you to meet his or her sexual needs. You may have been starving for attention, warmth, and affection. You may have been afraid of your family breaking up if you didn't go along with it, or if you told anyone. You may have been afraid that if you did tell someone you would not be believed. The perpetrator may have threatened to hurt you, your mother, siblings, your pets, or someone else you loved. You were not acting of your own free will.

For those in doubt as to whether they were abused and for those who doubt whether they still suffer from any damage from the abuse, consult the following list of long-term symptoms. While all victims experience difficulties in each of the broad categories listed, not every victim suffers from all the symptoms sublisted *under* each category. For example, all victims experience relationship problems, but not all are necessarily addicted to destructive relationships.

Most victims grow up to suffer from the following problems:

1. Damage to self-esteem and self-image.
2. Relationship problems.
3. Sexual problems.
4. Difficulties in expressing emotions.
5. Psychologically based physical symptoms and illnesses.

As we examine each category, check off those which you most identify with.

Damage to Self-Esteem and Self-Image

Even if the abused child starts out with high self-esteem (which is rare, since it is often children with low self-esteem who are abused in the first place), that esteem will be considerably lowered by the assault. Sexual abuse makes a child feel like "used property" or "damaged goods." Sexual abuse also causes a child to feel "bad," "sinful," and "evil," since there is inevitable self-blame. The victimization itself causes a child to lose feelings of personal power, since someone so young is so utterly helpless in that situation. And there is further shame about his or her body, especially if there was any physical arousal.

Long-Term Symptoms

- Feeling ugly inside.
- Feelings of worthlessness.
- Feeling that you are in the way.
- A tendency to overapologize and be overly solicitous to the point of making others angry.

- Feeling that you are stupid, a failure, a loser.
- Guilt feelings and feelings of shame.
- Tendency to blame yourself for whatever goes wrong.
- Inability to complete tasks.
- A tendency to sabotage success. (Victims often do not believe they *deserve* good things.)
- Tendency to be victimized by others.
- Feelings of helplessness.

Relationship Problems

More times than not, the perpetrator is someone known to the child—someone the child loves and trusts. The perpetrator betrays this trust by lying, coercing, and manipulating the child into doing things that hurt, humiliate, and frighten her or him. It is no wonder, then, that victims have a difficult time as adults trusting others. Because the relationship with the perpetrator was based on manipulation, deception, lies, and secrecy, a terrible foundation is established on which to build later relationships. One person had the *control,* and that person's needs were considered more important than those of the one *being* controlled. For this reason, closeness all too often comes to mean suffocation and entrapment.

Long-Term Symptoms

- Difficulty trusting others.
- Being distant, aloof.
- Tendency to be involved with destructive people who abuse you physically, verbally, emotionally, or sexually. (This may be the victim's way of punishing herself for the abuse, or she may be repeating the pattern of abuse by being with people who are like her parents or the perpetrator.)
- Lack of empathy or concern for others. (Victims may be

so concerned with survival that they are unable to reach out to others or to notice other people's problems.)

- A deep sense of isolation.
- Difficulty with physical affection. Not wanting to be touched or hugged; inability to express physical affection. Fearful of others' motives or of being misunderstood when you are affectionate.
- Secrecy, evasiveness, and tendency to withhold information from others. Or the opposite, a tendency to "tell all." (Because victims had to "hold in" their terrible secret, they may now go to the opposite extreme of telling everyone their story, even when it is inappropriate.)
- A tendency to "give yourself away." This includes helping others so much that you become exhausted, depriving yourself to give to others, giving away your personal possessions, and becoming sexually involved with anyone who desires you.
- Difficulties with authority figures. Frequent problems with bosses, teachers, or leaders (people who often remind victims of abusive parents or the perpetrator).
- Difficulty communicating desires, thoughts, and feelings to others. This includes "being at a loss for words," stuttering, stammering, and being afraid to speak in front of groups. (Victims who were told to "keep quiet," to "not tell anyone what we're doing," now fear being punished when they try to open up and talk.)
- Difficulty receiving from others. This includes awkwardness in accepting presents, favors, or compliments. Or its opposite, expecting others to show their love by buying you presents or giving you money (not believing they care unless they do).

Sexual Problems

In most cases, the first sexual experience most victims had was the sexual abuse. Instead of being one of exploration and tenderness, this initiation was one of exploitation and violence. It is extremely difficult to overcome this violation and make sexuality a positive experience. Sexuality brings with it fear, pain, and anger, as each encounter may be accompanied by memories and flashbacks of the abuse and the abuser. In addition, because of the early age of sexualization and the negative circumstances surrounding it, there has been little opportunity to differentiate between love and sex, closeness and sex.

Long-Term Symptoms

- Lack of sexual desire or inhibition of sexual feelings. Inability to enjoy sex or to have an orgasm.
- Sexual dysfunctions such as vaginismus (an involuntary contraction of the vaginal muscles, making penetration difficult or impossible) and painful intercourse.
- Inability to enjoy certain types of sexuality (can't be penetrated but can engage in oral sex; can't be fondled but can be penetrated; can't be touched on certain parts of the body).
- Problems with sexual identity.
- Promiscuity; continuing to be a sexual object.
- Attraction to "illicit" sexual activities such as pornography and prostitution.
- Anger and disgust at any public (or media) display of affection, sexuality, nudity, or partial nudity.
- Sexual manipulation. This includes using seductiveness or other forms of sexual manipulation to get what you want in your marital, social, or business relationships. Sexualizing all relationships (which can cause victims to become sexual victimizers of their own or other people's children).
- Sexual addiction, wherein victims, sexualized early on, often become addicted to daily sex or masturbation as a way of alleviating anxiety and comforting themselves.

Emotional Problems

Victims of childhood sexual abuse have a difficult time understanding, acknowledging, and expressing their emotions. Being overwhelmed by their feelings, many victims suppress their emotions, resulting in severe depression. Other victims have a difficult time controlling their emotions, especially anger, and therefore become violent and abusive to themselves and others.

Long-Term Symptoms

- Intense anger and rage that sometimes burst out unexpectedly.
- Mood swings, ranging from deep depression to an overactive, manic state.
- Chronic depression, resulting in sleeping too much and feeling apathetic, lethargic, hopeless, and even suicidal.
- Dissociation, a "splitting off" from oneself that probably started as a protection from the pain and devastation of the sexual abuse. Time blockages ("forgotten" periods of time, lasting even years, that are blocked from memory) and feelings of numbness in various parts of the body or even the entire body are also signs of dissociation.
- Extreme fears or phobias, including claustrophobia; an inordinate fear of going to the doctor or dentist; fear of taking a bath or shower; fear of going to sleep, of going to sleep with the door open (or closed), or of sleeping with anyone; fear of using public rest rooms.
- Sleep disturbances: nightmares, insomnia, waking up at the same time every night. (Because sexual abuse often occurred at night, victims tend to go to bed in an anxious state.)
- Addiction to food, alcohol, or drugs. (These are often avoidance tactics, ways to elude feelings of anger, pain, and fear. They may have been originally introduced by the per-

petrator as a way for him to have more power over the victim.)

- Obsessive/compulsive behavior, as in obsessive thoughts or compulsive shopping, shoplifting, gambling, eating, or cleaning. (As with addictions, obsessions and compulsions are ways to elude emotions.)
- Eating disorders. These include anorexia (slow suicide, the need to disappear or be invisible); obesity (fear of being attractive, need to nurture self, need for extra padding as a cushion against getting hurt so much); and bulimia (need to be in control of what goes into and out of your body).
- Flashbacks, hallucinations, in which the victim is suddenly flooded with memories of the abuse, usually triggered by something in the present, such as smelling the same aftershave used by the perpetrator. These can be *visual* (envisioning the scene); *tactile* (vaginal, pelvic, or anal pain, tingling, gagging, or smothering feelings); or *auditory* (hearing somebody breathe, cry, snore). These flashbacks, which may become more intense over time, may cause fear, dizziness, or nausea.
- Abusive behavior. Physically, verbally, emotionally, or sexually abusing others (including your children or animals). (Victims of childhood sexual abuse are usually afraid to release their anger toward their abusers, and instead take it out on those weaker than themselves.)
- Self-destructive behavior. Suicide attempts (pills, razors and knives, reckless driving); self-mutilation (scratching or picking at skin, cutting self with razor); binging and purging; alcohol or drug abuse; compulsive gambling; destructive relationships. (Because of their guilt, shame, self-hatred, and unexpressed rage, victims continue to abuse themselves and their bodies.)

Physical Problems

Because the sexual assault was against the body, adults who were sexually abused as children frequently suffer from a series of psychologically based illnesses. In addition, their bodies continue to give them important messages about what the abuse was like and what their bodies need now in order to heal.

Long-Term Symptoms

- Somatic symptoms (real physical problems that are psychologically originated), including sore throats, difficulty swallowing, migraine headaches, unexplained vaginal or anal pain, frequent bladder and vaginal infections, skin disorders, numbness or tingling in legs or arms.

- Tendency to be accident-prone. Victims may unconsciously be punishing themselves by hitting their bodies against furniture, falling, dropping things on themselves, or burning themselves "accidentally."

If you found yourself saying, "That's me!" to many of these symptoms, and if you suspect you were abused, the chances are *very* high that you were a victim of childhood sexual abuse.

Recognizing how the abuse has affected you may be painful, but it is an important part of the healing process. This recognition can give you more of a sense of control, since self-knowledge can empower you and make you feel less confused, different, or "crazy."

Be reassured: Even though you have been suffering for a long time with little relief, there is hope for recovery, hope for healing. You now have an opportunity to benefit from the same survival and recovery program that others have followed successfully. You may have felt isolated with your pain, but you no longer have to be. Many others like you have suffered from the same pain, fear, and anger. You are not alone.

CHAPTER 2

Sexual Abuse: What It Is and What It's Not

CHILDREN WHO ARE sexually abused are told all kinds of lies. They are lied to by the perpetrator, who wants to convince them that it is okay for adults to have sex with children, that it is a good way to learn about sex, and that it is a normal way for an adult to show affection and love. Victims are also lied to by their families, who tell them that they are making it up, that the perpetrator did not mean any harm, or that he or she was just trying to be "friendly." And they are lied to by society, which is inclined to sweep childhood sexual abuse under the carpet.

Most adults have a difficult time accepting the fact that childhood sexual abuse occurs at all, much less to the extent that it does. So they treat it the same way they treat anything they don't want to face: They go into denial about it. The denial process is a defense mechanism against the truth. In regard to sexual abuse, people tend to resist dealing with the truth on many levels, denying that childhood sexual abuse exists at all; denying that it occurs as frequently as it does; denying that anyone *they* know is involved in it, either as victim or perpetrator; denying that it really harms the child (maybe it's actually good for the child, maybe it can help teach about sex); convincing themselves that a child will not remember it; denying that they sexually abused a child themselves; denying that they themselves were sexually abused.

Perpetrators confound the issue with their denial and dishonesty. A perpetrator will seldom, if ever, admit to having abused a child. If caught in the act, a perpetrator will likely blame someone else—usually the child—as did the father of one of my clients: "She would sit on my lap and wiggle around until I got an erection. What else could I do?" In a fairly recent case in California involving a school principal accused of sexually molesting and exposing himself to his students, the man protested, "I wouldn't have done it [admitting that he did indeed masturbate in front of a classroom of children] if they hadn't wanted me to." Most perpetrators are both manipulative and convincing, capable of expertly covering up their activities and charming and deceiving parents as well as children.

Thus evolves a vicious cycle obscuring the truth about childhood sexual abuse: Perpetrators lie about it, silent partners and family members ignore it, and victims repress it. As a result, victims often have a difficult time perceiving exactly what the truth is. Moreover, a great deal of misinformation abounds on the topic. This is dangerous; it keeps victims imprisoned in their symptoms and by their families.

In order to clear up some of this confusion, we will examine some common myths about childhood sexual abuse and counter them with facts—facts that have been validated by research, hundreds of clients' experiences, and this author's own clinical work. We will focus on the abuse itself, the perpetrator, and the victim.

MYTHS ABOUT INCEST

MYTH: Sex between members of the same family has been widely accepted for centuries. It is only recently that people see it as unacceptable.
FACT: On the contrary, throughout history, sex between members of the same nuclear family has been outlawed and restricted. This prohibition is called the *incest taboo.*

The incest taboo, widely believed to be universal, is one of the cornerstones of Judeo-Christian morality. Admittedly, in rare cases, some primitive societies temporarily suspend the incest ban and allow certain kinds of incestuous relations in the context of magical rituals. But accounts of these exceptions are often exaggerated. Even so, primitive societies also practice other rituals we would find unacceptable, such as rubbing the body with the urine of the sacred cow, putting bones in noses, or eating the limb of a live animal, as some tribes in Africa do.

MYTH: The incest taboo refers only to *marriage* between family members; if there is no marriage and there are no offspring, there is no need for an incest taboo.
FACT: The purpose of the incest taboo is the preservation of the family unit and the protection of the children in particular.

Many people assume that the purpose of the incest taboo is to prevent close inbreeding, which can result in congenital malformations. But the incest taboo in Western culture precedes the science of genetics. Genetics has only been considered a science since the early 1900s but we have had the incest taboo since the time of Christ. Evidence indicates that the incest taboo insures a healthy environment for children, since the family's primary role is that of socializing children. If, for example, we consider the possessiveness and jealousy that so often characterizes the sexual attachment between two people, imagine the chaos possible by promiscuous sex within a family.

Moreover, the incest taboo forces family members to seek partners outside the family, so that the community will broaden its ties and grow stronger. It also forces people to become psychologically independent of the family—to become individuals. The emotional bonds between parent and child are difficult to break. If sexual bonds are also made, the tie between parent and child (or siblings) becomes much more difficult to sever.

MYTH: There is no perpetrator when it comes to sibling incest.
FACT: Sibling incest can be as traumatic as incest between parent and child.

Even a one-year age difference between siblings has enormous power implications for both parties. For example, an older brother is almost always seen as the authority figure, even when he is only a few years older. The sister goes along with it out of fear or out of a need to please. There are also cases where the older sister is the aggressor, although this does not happen quite as often. The greater the age difference, the greater the betrayal of trust, and the more violent the incest tends to be.

Normal sex play and exploration can occur only between those of the same age, sexual experience, and power. "Playing doctor" between consenting age peers is likely to represent normal sexual experimentation, while sexual activity between a young child and an adolescent most likely represents sexual abuse.

Only under certain specific circumstances is sibling incest *not* sexual abuse:

1. The children are young and approximately the same age.
2. They each have equal power, both with each other and in the family.
3. There is no betrayal of trust between them. This would be possible only if they were of the same age and each had equal power.
4. There is no coercion or physical force.
5. The sexual play is the result of natural curiosity, exploration, and mutual sexual naiveté.
6. The children are not traumatized by disapproving parents who may "catch them in the act."

MYTHS ABOUT CHILDHOOD SEXUAL ABUSE

MYTH: The whole issue of childhood sexual abuse has been blown out of porportion. There isn't that much sexual abuse going on today or in the past.
FACT: Childhood sexual abuse is pervasive in spite of the universal ban on incest.

With one in three girls and one in seven boys being sexually molested before the age of eighteen in this country, sexual abuse is emerging as an epidemic form of child abuse. Ten years ago, sexual abuse was considered a relatively uncommon problem. But in the late 1970s, official reports of childhood sexual abuse increased at a rate that dwarfed reports of other forms of abuse. In spite of this increase, studies suggest that sexual abuse is still largely underreported.

Diana Russell's study of 930 San Francisco women in 1979 found that 38 percent of those questioned had been sexually victimized. Other surveys have found similarly high rates of sexual victimization. Sociologist David Finkelhor, in his 1979 sample of 796 college students, found that 19 percent of the females and 9 percent of the males had been sexually abused.

The current flood of reports of childhood sexual abuse in the United States has caused many people to wonder whether sexual abuse is on the rise. It is more probable that people's current willingness to report what was previously an unmentionable experience accounts for the increase.

MYTH: It is acceptable for an adult to have sex with a child so long as the child is not a relative. This practice has been going on for centuries.
FACT: It is no more acceptable for an adult to have sex with an unrelated child than it is for him to have sex with a relative.

Child abuse (including sexual abuse) has been recorded throughout written history. In the early days of civilization, children were viewed as property, to be disposed of in whatever way the parent or guardian saw fit. Infants were killed for being deformed, unwanted, or the wrong sex. Given this mentality about the dispensability of children, it can be easily assumed that all types of child abuse may have been prevalent over history. In the Victorian era, for example, many kinds of sexual perversity prevailed, especially concerning the sexual abuse of children. Large numbers of children populated the brothels of Europe, a thriving international sex-slave market trafficked in children, and there were numerous sex crimes against children.

In the last few decades, however, growing public awareness has forced us to admit that although childhood sexual abuse still occurs, it is utterly wrong. A child's immature intellectual and emotional structure is not equipped for a sexual awakening, and sexual abuse can damage him or her for life.

MYTH: There is no difference between child marriages in history and sex between adults and children today.
FACT: There are two obvious differences: First, the intention of historical child marriages was to benefit society; and second, the practice was sanctioned by the entire society.

Until approximately the last fifty years in parts of the United States and right up to the present time in many Third World countries, adolescent girls of twelve to sixteen years of age routinely wed men of thirty or older. This practice, however, served a social function, because of the scarcity of women of childbearing age and because many women did not live past the age of thirty. This is no longer the case. Indeed, it is well documented that girls who give birth during their puberty years are at a higher risk of having deformed or retarded babies or of having complicated births.

In our society today, having sex with a child serves no social function. It is an act of selfishness that is almost always surrounded by an atmosphere of secrecy.

MYTH: Childhood sexual abuse involves intercourse by an adult with a child. If there is no penetration, the act is not considered sexual abuse.
FACT: Many forms of sexual abuse do not involve intercourse or any kind of penetration.

Below is an abbreviated version of a list that originally appeared in *Handbook of Clinical Intervention in Child Sexual Abuse* by Suzanne M. Sgroi (Lexington, Mass.: Lexington Books, 1982). The list contains many of the types of sexual abuse toward children of either sex:

1. *Nudity.* The adult parades around the house in front of all or some of the family members.

2. *Disrobing.* The adult disrobes in front of the child, generally when the child and the adult are alone.
3. *Genital exposure.* The adult exposes his or her genitals to the child.
4. *Observation of the child.* The adult surreptitiously or overtly watches the child undress, bathe, excrete, or urinate.
5. *Kissing.* The adult kisses the child in a lingering or intimate way.
6. *Fondling.* The adult fondles the child's breasts, abdomen, genital area, inner thighs, or buttocks. The child may similarly fondle the adult at his or her request.
7. *Masturbation.* The adult masturbates while the child observes; the adult observes the child masturbating; the adult and child masturbate each other (mutual masturbation).
8. *Fellatio.* The adult has the child fellate him or her, or the adult fellates the child.
9. *Cunnilingus.* This type of oral-genital contact requires either the child to place mouth and tongue on the vulva or in the vaginal area of an adult female or the adult to place his or her mouth on the vulva or in the vaginal area of the female child.
10. *Digital (finger) penetration of the anus or rectal opening.* Perpetrators may also thrust inanimate objects such as crayon or pencils inside.
11. *Penile penetration of the anus or rectal opening.*
12. *Digital (finger) penetration of the vagina.* Inanimate objects may also be inserted.
13. *"Dry intercourse."* A slang term describing an interaction in which the adult rubs his penis against the child's genital-rectal area or inner thighs or buttocks.
14. *Penile penetration of the vagina.*

Although this list *seems* to increase in severity, it is important to remember that *all* types of sexual abuse, even nudity and kissing, can be emotionally and psychologically damaging to a child. Keep in mind that the *intention* of the adult or older child while engaging in some of the earlier acts (nudity, disrobing, observation of the child, and so on) will determine whether the act is actually sexually abusive. If an adult watches a child bathe, for example, but does so in a *nonsexual* way that does not upset the child, it may not be sexually abusive. But if the adult becomes sexually aroused while watching, it is then sexual abuse.

If *any* of the above-listed acts took place in infancy, childhood, or adolescence with someone older, and the child felt uncomfortable or strange about it, then she or he was sexually abused. Of equal importance is any indirect or direct sexual suggestion made by an adult toward a child. This is called *approach behavior.* It can include sexual looks, innuendos, or suggestive gestures. Even if the adult never engaged in touching or took any overt sexual action, the sexual feelings that are projected are picked up by the child.

MYTH: Adults need to teach children about sex so they will grow up to be good lovers.
FACT: The opposite is true. Children who were sexually abused grow up to be adults who suffer from many sexual problems.

Victims report feeling stigmatized and confused about sexual and nonsexual encounters, being involved with compulsive sexual activity, or wanting to avoid all sexual activity. In the book *By Silence Betrayed* by John Crewdson, several surveys revealed these figures: Two hundred prostitutes were interviewed in four cities. In San Francisco, 60 percent had histories of childhood sexual abuse. In New York City, it was 75 percent; in Seattle, 65 percent; and in San Diego, 90 percent. The dangerous, worn-out rationalization many perpetrators use that "it will make you a better lover when you grow up" has absolutely no grounds in research or reality.

Children need their developmental years in which to play and grow freely, unencumbered by sex. They need their time of innocence to mature and develop emotionally and sexually at their own speed. Then, as young adults ready to learn about sex, they can embark on that adventure with age-appropriate sex partners of their own choice.

MYTH: Sexual abuse doesn't really cause any damage to the child as long as there is no violence or pain.
FACT: There is always harm and pain, even if it is emotional rather than physical.

Evidence reveals that childhood sexual abuse of any kind results in emotional and psychological damage lasting a lifetime. As mentioned above, children need time to be children before they are capable of handling any sexual relationship. Sexuality foisted upon them too early amounts to abuse, and it is still abuse even in the complete absence of physical pain.

MYTHS ABOUT THE PERPETRATORS

MYTH: Most child molesters are strangers.
FACT: The majority of abusers are relatives, most notably stepfathers, fathers, uncles, brothers, and grandfathers.

When asked to describe a sexual abuser, many people still think in terms of a stranger. Still others have the stereotypical image of the "dirty old man" in a raincoat who hangs around the schoolyard, offering candy.

Few people realize that the majority of abusers are in fact relatives. Eighty-five percent of childhood sexual abuse occurs in the home. David Finkelhor, in his book *Child Sexual Abuse: New Theory and Research,* noted that having a stepfather constitutes one of the strongest risk factors, more than doubling a girl's chance of being sexually molested. Moreover, his study reveals that a stepfather is five times more likely to sexually victimize a daughter than is a natural father.

Who are these perpetrators? Offenders are most likely to be young and middle-aged adults. According to Finkelhor, over 90 percent of them are men. However, not all incestuous abuse is necessarily perpetrated by adults. In *The Secret Trauma,* Diana Russell's study of female incest victims, 26 percent of the cases involved perpetrators who were under eighteen years of age, and 15 percent of the incest perpetrators were less than five years older than their victims.

MYTH: A father who "loses control" and molests his daughter is not as bad as the child molester who goes around stalking children.
FACT: The incest offender is often just a child molester who stays home.

Father-daughter incest is considered by most experts to be the most traumatic form of incestuous abuse, and incestuous abuse is considered the most traumatic form of childhood sexual abuse. There is general agreement that the roots of incestuous assault are to be found in feelings of anger, insecurity, and isolation harbored by the aggressor. A father who molests his daughter may blame it on the victim or his wife, stress at work, his alcohol abuse, his unemployment, or a myriad of other "causes," but the truth is that the problem resides in himself as a result of deviant arousal and will travel with him wherever he goes. If you put him in another family, the molestation would still take place. In this sense, he is no different from any other child molester.

MYTH: A man sexually abuses children because he is not getting his sexual and emotional needs met by his wife.
FACT: Childhood sexual abuse, like rape, is an act of violence and anger, not of sex.

Aggressors rarely commit childhood sexual abuse to satisfy purely sexual needs. Instead, they do it to meet a number of emotional needs: to exercise power over someone; to seek revenge against a wife or mother for what he considers neglectful or abusive treatment; or to seek from the child that which he lacks so desperately in himself. Many child molesters are in fact unable to maintain a sexual relationship with an adult woman because of overriding feelings of inadequacy and insecurity.

MYTH: Child molesters, many of whom were themselves abused as children, are emotionally disturbed; they are therefore not responsible for their behavior.
FACT: Some professionals do consider child molesters to be emotionally disturbed, but at no time are they rendered incapable of assuming responsibility for their actions.

In psychotherapeutic jargon, many child molesters suffer from a disorder called pedophilia, a specific combination of "deviant arousal" and "character disorder." In lay terms, this means the molester is both sexually excited by children and sees nothing wrong with gratifying himself at their expense. Although there is a consensus among the experts that pedophiles do not consciously choose to be attracted to children, they do choose to *act* on their urges. No matter how much he may himself have been deprived or victimized, the child molester is still responsible for his actions. People who are sexually attracted to children do not have to act on it. There are several options: to make certain never to be left alone with a child; to seek professional help; to warn other family members of the attraction.

It is true that the majority of perpetrators were sexually abused as children. Such victimization is believed to underlie the attraction to and victimization of children. But victimizing helpless children does *not* undo the childhood trauma. There is no excuse for continuing the cycle of abuse, and not all victims of childhood sexual abuse necessarily repeat the pattern. Consider, for example, that women rarely molest children, even though more girls are molested than boys. Many victims, such as yourself, seek help in order *not* to continue the cycle.

Some argue that the child molester is out of control, that he has a compulsion to sexually abuse children, just as some people have a compulsion to drink or overeat. Child molesters are out of control and they do need help. But we must not fall into the trap of excusing their behavior on these grounds. One thing that is brought out over and over while talking to perpetrators is that they did know right from wrong, they did know they needed help, but they chose not to get it. They are generally more bent on denying responsibility for their actions and finding ways of continuing their behavior than they are on seeking help.

Child molesters generally fall into one of two categories: the sociopath and the self-deceiver. The sociopath has no moral qualms about hurting others to get what he wants. He simply doesn't have any regard for others' feelings. He seems to have his own set of values that do not correspond to society's values. This character disorder is manifested by a lack of empathy for the victim, little regard for social taboos, and poor impulse control.

The self-deceiver, on the other hand, minimizes the harm he causes and projects the blame onto the victim or his wife. He employs defense mechanisms to keep a grip on his sanity.

Defense mechanisms are normal, but offenders use them in excessive ways.

There seem to be three distinct types of sex offenders:

1. Those with major psychiatric disorders (schizophrenia, manic-depressive illness, organic brain syndrome). This group makes up the smallest proportion of offenders.
2. Those with an antisocial personality disorder (sociopaths). These offenders have long histories of poor impulse control, poor social relationships, and behaviors that violate laws and acceptable community values and standards.
3. Those who are pedophiles. Pedophilia is characterized by compulsive thoughts and urges to engage in sexually deviant behaviors. It is believed that pedophiles learn their deviant sexual behaviors through observation and/or direct experience (sexual victimization). Pedophiles represent the largest proportion of child sexual abusers.

MYTH: Just because a man makes a mistake and molests one child doesn't mean he will do it again with other children.
FACT: Rare is the offender who molests once and then stops.

Like an addict, he quickly becomes hooked. If anything, the molester's sexual activity accelerates rather than dissipates after the first incident. The attempts often become more brash, the abuses occur more frequently, and the acts become more intrusive. The compulsion to repeat the sexual abuse is so great that the behavior is likely to continue even after he has been caught. Child molesters go to great lengths and put a vast amount of energy, time, and effort into maintaining their behavior, much like any addict. Many seek jobs, hobbies, and volunteer activities that involve youngsters. The incestuous stepfather who molests his stepchildren is likely to have abused other children outside the relationship and may even have married the woman because she had children.

MYTH: Child molesters can be "cured."
FACT: Unless the perpetrator openly admits his actions and takes responsibility, there is little hope for change.

With rare exception, most aggressors do not admit their responsibility for the sexual abuse. Denial is the most common reaction; the second reaction is to blame either the child or his wife. Even those who do admit being the seducer do not accept responsibility for the incidents.

Statistics indicate that few child molesters voluntarily seek help. People don't give up pleasurable behavior that brings a very powerful payoff unless there's a compelling reason to do so. Some experts believe that legal prosecution is absolutely necessary to force these people to follow through with therapy. The molester must admit the gravity of his offense and let down his armor of rationalization. Then he must work on his problem every day for the rest of his life, much like a recovered alcoholic. Many authorities believe that sex offenders can never be cured and can learn only to control their sexually deviant behavior.

There is a poor prognosis for recovery for all three types of child molester. Those with psychiatric disorders may need hospitalization and/or medication, which could reduce the possibility of further childhood sexual abuse.

Recovery for the sociopathic (antisocial) types of perpetrators is even more rare, since they seldom believe that what they did was wrong.

The third type of offender, the pedophile, is generally considered to be "incurable." This is especially true of those whose primary sexual attraction and orientation is to children. Sexual preference is not something one can easily change. The best that can be hoped for is that such behavior can be *controlled.*

From my own clinical experience, the only time a child molester seems to have any hope for recovery is when he not only admits to himself that he has a problem but when he also admits it to others. It is especially important to admit to his family and to the victim that he was entirely responsible for the abuse. Even though it is extremely rare for a child molester to recognize and assume full responsibility for the pain and suffering he has inflicted, *if* he is sincere in his admittance of guilt, *if* he asks the victim for forgiveness and offers real assurance that she or he was not responsible in any way, and *if* he commits himself to change through therapy or self-help groups like Parents United, there is some hope for real change.

MYTH: Childhood sexual abuse by females does not occur.
FACT: Most sexual offenses against children are perpetrated by males, but some abuse by females does occur and should not be overlooked.

Mother-son incest is probably the most subtly traumatic of all forms of incest. Since the incestuous mother cannot easily force her son, she must use seductiveness. This seductiveness turns out to be deadly, since the boy can't help but respond and then feels horribly guilty afterward. The long-term effects of this kind of abuse range from impotency to self-destructiveness. The victim, usually resentful of women, often becomes a child molester, a wife beater, a rapist, or even a murderer.

Mothers who sexually abuse their daughters are emotionally disturbed and often psychotic. Many of them were sexually abused as children and thus feel "dirty" inside because of their shame. They project these bad feelings onto their daughters, whom they also see as bad and dirty. They see their daughters as extensions of themselves. They may stimulate their daughters sexually in order to satisfy their own needs for pleasure. These women, emotionally isolated as children, never learned to express affection appropriately. They may actually believe that their actions are demonstrations of affection.

Male clients have often told me with something approaching pride about their first sexual experiences with a female baby-sitter. As we work together, however, they begin to recognize the damage that such early sexualization can cause.

MYTHS ABOUT THE VICTIMS

MYTH: There is no such thing as a true victim. The child has some responsibility in the situation.
FACT: The child is totally innocent and has absolutely *no* responsibility for the sexual abuse.

One of the most common and effective ways in which people deny the seriousness of childhood sexual abuse is to blame the victim. In this way, those who want to avoid facing the truth about childhood sexual abuse can deceive themselves into thinking that there was really no victim at all. This tendency to blame the victim is so pervasive that most child-victims come to believe that they really were at fault in some way. This sense of guilt and responsibility is carried into adulthood.

MYTH: The child could have stopped it at any time.
FACT: There is no way a child can stop an adult from doing what he or she wants with her.

A child is not physically strong enough to push an adult away, nor is a child emotionally or intellectually mature enough to outsmart an adult. Child molesters are very good "con men," and a child is no match for their clever manipulation. In addition, they may threaten to hurt the child or someone the child loves; they may tell the child he or she will be punished if anyone finds out; or they may convince the child that "everyone does it." Children are taught to obey adults; thus, they feel they have no choice.

MYTH: All the child had to do was to run away.
FACT: There was no place to go.

Since most childhood sexual abuse occurs at home, running away would mean running away from *home.* Where would a child run to, being totally dependent upon family for survival? No matter how bad it is at home, a child still feels safer being with parents than being without them. Familiarity, however miserable, is preferred over the unknown.

MYTH: All the child had to do to stop it was to tell someone.
FACT: A child is too *afraid* to tell.

As we mentioned earlier, there are many reasons why sexually abused children don't tell:

- They have been threatened by their abuser, who they fear may kill them, their parents, or their pets.
- They are afraid that no one will believe them. They may already have had the experience of telling their parents the truth, only to be accused of making it up. They believe that their word alone would very likely not be honored.
- They are afraid they will be blamed.
- They are afraid they will be punished. Children who are

sexually abused often have a history of being severely punished for even the slightest mistake. They are therefore much more inclined to keep quiet about something so awful, which is bound to result in commensurate punishment.

- They feel there is no use in telling. If their parents are rarely around or are usually overinvolved in their own lives, children may feel that their parents simply don't care what happens to them.
- They feel such guilt and shame that they just can't tell. This is especially true if their body responded to the sexual stimulation. They fear that anyone they might tell would surely blame them as much as they blame themselves.
- They feel that somehow their mother must already know about what is going on, and therefore they feel too betrayed to tell.
- They may have been afraid their mother would divorce their father (the abuser) if they told. Many victims fear being sent to a foster home.
- They may be protecting the perpetrator, keeping the secret for the sake of a parent or someone else the child loves.

MYTH: Children often go back for more. How bad could it be?
FACT: Children continue to be around the perpetrator because they are getting some of their *other* needs met. They just put up with the sex.

There may be some aspects that the children needed and desired—the attention, the holding, the compliments—because they were not getting these needs met elsewhere. Children do *not* go back for the sex. They want to believe that adults (especially adults they love and trust) are good, kind, and caring. To children, an adult who loves them would not hurt them. If an adult *does* do something to hurt them (such as sexually molesting them), then children turn the blame and responsibility onto themselves. They think perhaps they weren't lovable or "good" enough to deserve continual love from the adult, and so they keep going back, hoping to be good enough so that maybe the adult will stop hurting them. Children also learn to deny their emotional and physical pain. They convince themselves that perhaps the abuser will not ever do it again.

MYTH: Some children really want it. They get physical pleasure from it.
FACT: No matter how their *body* responds, a child does not want to have sex with an adult.

Some victims of childhood sexual abuse talk about how their bodies *betrayed* them, responding to the sexual stimulation even while they resisted in their minds. That does not mean they "enjoyed" it, or that they wanted it. Our bodies can indeed respond without our consent.

MYTH: Some of these victims were old enough to know better. In these cases it is not sexual abuse.
FACT: It is considered childhood sexual abuse if the victim was coerced, deceived, threatened, bribed, or intimidated. When sexual encounters are not based on mutual consent, they always constitute assault.

A child under the age of eighteen is not old enough to "consent" to having sex with an adult or even someone more than a few years older, because there is a difference in power. In order for true consent to occur, the person must know what it is that he or she is consenting to, *and* must have true freedom to say yes or no. Children lack the information necessary to make an "informed" decision about the matter and do not have the personal freedom, nor power or position, to say yes or no to an adult, especially if that adult controls all their means for survival.

Generally, children under the age of sixteen and sometimes older are not emotionally equipped to have sex with anyone, much less with an adult or a much older adolescent. If a parent or parental figure, an older sibling, or any other family member wants to have sex with a child under the age of eighteen, the child is never old enough to "know better."

MYTH: Some children are just asking for trouble. That is why some kids have it happen to them over and over.
FACT: Abusers "pick" whoever is around, available, or convenient, often choosing a child who has previously been sexually victimized.

Abusers tend to find children who are vulnerable. They have an uncanny knack for singling out children who have already been victimized in some way (physically, verbally, or emotionally) and can spot the child who is hungry for love, attention, and affection. Once a child has been sexually abused, he or she is an easy target for other child molesters. The previously victimized child has low self-esteem and tends to submit more willingly to advances. On the other hand, a previously victimized child may appear to be sexual in the way she stands, sits, or moves, or may have learned to be seductive in order to get attention.

The child who is protected and supervised by her family, especially by her mother, is not easy prey. But children whose mothers are physically or psychologically absent are more vulnerable. Children who live in isolated settings or who have few friends and few social contacts are also at greater risk.

MYTH: Some children are naturally oversexed.

FACT: Children who have already been victimized often act in provocative ways in order to get attention.

A so-called precocious, provocative, or seductive child appears so because of *prior* sexual abuse. This behavior reveals that the child has already been sexualized, that he or she has already been introduced to sex and has "learned" that acting seductive can be an effective way to get the affection, attention, and approval that are so badly needed.

The abuser teaches his victims a powerful but dysfunctional message—that they are important because of their sexuality. Sex becomes a tool that is used to manipulate others. Ironically, however, these children are even more desperate for love after the abuse than they were before. Since most victims of childhood sexual abuse do not tell anyone about the trauma they have been through, there is no one to comfort them. They feel alone and scared, with nowhere to turn for solace. So they look for reassurance and comfort anywhere they can find it—even if it means being abused again (sometimes by the same person).

CHAPTER 3

Reaching Out, Reaching In

IF YOU CAN find the courage to reach out for help, there is hope. Yet reaching out for help can be very difficult for victims of childhood sexual abuse. First of all, as a victim you learned various survival skills in order to cope with the sexual abuse. *Denial* is one of the most common of them. You may have denied your pain, denied that you were damaged by the abuse, or denied that you are still suffering from it. Giving up this denial is frightening, because it will mean that you will have to face the pain all over again.

Reaching out for help is also difficult because you have learned to protect yourself from further hurt and abuse by not trusting anyone. Adults who were molested as children still feel isolated and different many years after the incident(s). Although they may be aware of self-help groups, they often refrain from attending them. Many are also reluctant to go to a therapist for fear of being disbelieved, further exploited, or "analyzed and shrunk."

Generally speaking, men are particularly reluctant to seek therapy, and even those who do are often unable to tell their therapist they were sexually abused for fear of being judged. Males are sometimes more damaged from the sexual abuse than females and can suffer even more long-term effects. Males are not used to being victims or of being seen as victims in our society, and so they suffer further guilt and shame over having been a victim at all.

Some women also have difficulty reaching out for help. They have put up a façade of being strong, independent, and self-sufficient, but they don't ask for help—in fact, they are usually the ones who help everyone else. Although others may not see their pain and suffering, it remains there, just under the surface. You alone know if you are one of these women; you alone know if you need help or not. And only you know whether you are ready to seek this help.

If you are ready and willing to reach out for help, it is available. In addition to following the program outlined in this book, I strongly urge you to either join a support group or enter individual therapy. A support group will offer you the chance to discover that there are others who share your feelings, and it will provide you the opportunity to get valuable support, feedback, and suggestions as you work through the program. It will also provide a safe place to express the feelings that will surface as an inevitable part of the healing process. These days, nearly every town across the nation has a support group for victims of childhood sexual abuse. Up until only a few years ago, this was not the case. Especially in rural areas and small towns, survivors had no one to turn to. They assumed they were the only ones to have been abused. Today we know this is not true. With so many victims of child abuse now coming forward, you can be assured that there are *many* other victims in your area and that there is more than likely a self-help or support group available.

Referral sources for support groups are listed in the back of this book. If for some reason you cannot find a group, consider starting your own, using this book as a guide. Put up a notice at your church or social club, or advertise in your local paper. You will be surprised at the number of people who may respond.

In addition to a support group, you may wish to consider individual therapy with a professional who specializes in helping childhood sexual abuse victims recover. Individual therapy will provide you with the opportunity to develop a trusting, honest, healthy relationship—perhaps for the first time. If cost is a factor, consider the services available at your local community mental health clinic, which provides inexpensive individual therapy on a sliding-scale basis.

Of course, the most effective option is to do all of the above. This book is intended to be an *adjunct* to therapy or a support group. It will offer you specific techniques that you won't learn in counseling or in a twelve-step Alcoholics Anonymous–type program. With the added help of this book, you can work on your recovery program as often as you like. This can speed your recovery tremendously. If you are not ready to seek outside help, go ahead with your own process with the aid of this book. Follow the steps, perhaps using a special friend for emotional support when you need it. You can reconsider seeking help at any time, as soon as you are ready.

Immense courage and much work is required on your part to recover from the childhood experience of sexual abuse. There are no quick solutions, no simple steps or techniques. Each step in this book will take time, and the process will sometimes seem endless, the pain sometimes overwhelming. But it is worth all the time, pain, and hard work. You will be rewarded with freedom from the anger, fear, and pain of the past and with the ability to have true control over your life. You will have a more positive self-image, a newfound confidence, and the ability to trust others and yourself. You will also have improved relationships, a healthy sex life, and the capacity to more fully love yourself and others.

TELLING YOUR STORY

As part of accepting your desire to recover, it is important that you tell your story in all its painful detail. Much as this may hurt, it will be a tremendous release. It will help you to remember things you have forgotten or blocked out, to break through your denial and force you to admit it really happened. Telling your story will make it more real. There is relief in knowing that you did not make it up, that you are not crazy.

Be careful whom you tell—but do tell someone. Generally speaking, the safest people to tell will be a therapist or the other members of a support group. They will understand and be supportive and will assure you that it's not your fault, that you aren't the crazy one, and that you aren't a liar. If your therapist implies that perhaps you *were* to blame or had some responsibility for it, or maybe that it couldn't have been *that* bad, you are with the wrong therapist.

If you aren't in therapy or in a group, tell your mate or your closest friend. He or she may not be as understanding but will probably try to be supportive. Most people do become very uncomfortable with this subject, and they may not know what to say or do. Just say that all you need is to be listened to and not criticized and that the perpetrator not be defended—no matter who it is. If you just can't tell *anyone* yet, then write your story down. This will help unburden you of your secret and remind you that it really did happen. Perhaps you can even allow someone to read it when you are ready.

Shelley's older brother Tom started molesting her when she was eight years old and he was eleven. Although there was not a great age difference between them, the fact that Tom used coercion and threats to get Shelley to cooperate made his advances abusive. Shelley was afraid of him because he was constantly beating her. Her parents never punished

Tom for hitting her, but instead would reprimand Shelly for "making him angry." She suspected her parents would reject her story about the sexual abuse. Practicing Catholics, she was sure they would be too deeply shocked to "believe" it. She feared they would see her as the temptress, since that is how they seemed to view all females.

Her assumptions were correct. One night her father walked in on them. He turned around and left without saying a word. And the next morning he had *Shelley* go to confession. Nothing was ever said to her brother. The abuse continued for nine more years, until she was seventeen years old and moved out of the house. Although she felt terrorized each time he entered her room, she eventually began to respond to his touch. The only time he was gentle or affectionate with her was when he was being sexual with her. Otherwise, he continued to physically and verbally abuse her.

Because she responded to his touches, and because the molestation continued for so long, Shelley became convinced that her parents must be right—she must be the evil one. And as time went on she became more and more confused about what the truth really was. When Shelley started therapy with me she was convinced that she had instigated the incest, that she was a liar and an evil temptress who didn't deserve to live. She had carried around the secret of the incest all her life, never telling anyone for fear of being judged. She was afraid no one in the support group would believe her, that they would all think she was sick for having "enjoyed" it.

When other group members told her *it wasn't her fault,* she broke down and cried. No one had ever told her that *anything* was not her fault before. When two other women in the group shared that they too had been sexually abused by their older brothers, she felt tremendous relief that she was not the "only one." This was the beginning of Shelley's recovery.

REACHING IN

In addition to reaching out for help, you will also need to reach within yourself during your recovery process. Your biggest ally will be your emotions. Through them, you will learn more about what really happened to you, how the abuse affected you, and what you need to do in order to heal. Your emotions will enable you to reclaim the self you long ago hid away.

Typically, victims of childhood sexual abuse have a difficult time expressing their feelings. They are more accustomed to minimizing their pain and hiding how they really feel, both from themselves and from others. They often become frightened whenever they feel *anything* intensely, be it anger, pain, fear, or even love and joy. They fear that their emotions will consume them or make them crazy. They imagine their emotions spilling out, creating havoc in their lives.

But the more repressed our feelings, the more likely that they will burst out of us when we least expect it. Strong feelings repressed for too long become uncontainable; they can result in our overreacting or reacting inappropriately, our becoming irrational or being prone to "temper tantrums." You will not "go crazy" if you allow yourself to feel and express your strong emotions. On the contrary, you are more likely to have emotional disorders from resisting, denying, and *not* expressing your feelings. If you consistently and constructively express your feelings as they occur, instead of holding them in, then a sense of personal power results. You will find that you are *more* in control of your emotions, not less.

WHY WE COME TO DENY OUR FEELINGS

Victims of childhood sexual abuse have been taught by their parents to suppress and deny their feelings. Usually, at least one parent was very out of touch with his or her own feelings. This nonexpressive, nonaffectionate parent would discourage any overt display of emotion in the household. As a child you may have also been told, "You're too sensitive," or, "You feel too strongly about things."

Children learn to deny their personal feelings when they live in a home in which everyone is busy ignoring the reality of how bad things really are. Even before the sexual abuse occurred, you may have been physically, emotionally, or verbally abused by one or both of your parents or caretakers. Time after time, you may have been told that nothing had happened, even though you knew it had.

As Sandra told her support group: "My parents would have these horrible fights. They would keep us awake half of the night with their screaming. The next morning my mother's face would be bruised and battered. She would tell everyone that she had 'run into a door.' "

Margaret added her own version: "My mother had what everyone called 'spells.' She would go around the house muttering to herself, looking right through me as if I weren't there. She would dress up in weird outfits and dance by herself to imaginary music. Then she would break out into these bloodcurdling screams and lock herself up in her room for days at a time. Our entire family denied that she needed psychiatric help, even though she had episode after episode of this insane behavior." Soon Sandra and Margaret were joined by nearly everyone else in the group, with similar stories to tell.

With this kind of denial of reality going on in the home, it is no wonder we grew up not being able to trust our own feelings and perceptions. When the sexual abuse began, we were again told that nothing was wrong. Swayed by the smooth-talking adult, we began to deny our body signals, dismissed our doubts and fears, and ultimately complied. In addition, we very likely began to master "spacing out" (splitting or dissociating) to avoid pain. Eventually we called on it to cope with any painful situation. We buffered ourselves from the world, operating as if in a fog. As a result, when we became adults we found ourselves seldom completely mentally and emotionally present when interacting with others. Unfortunately, this survival mechanism served to exclude us from being in the real world, from learning how to relate successfully to others; we thus became isolated and disconnected from others and ourselves.

Some survivors pride themselves at their ability to withstand physical pain; they see it as a sign of strength. They "keep going," in spite of injuries, illnesses, and symptoms that would otherwise sideline most people. This ability to ignore pain contributes to the delusion that other problems will also go away if only ignored long enough. The price to be paid for all this avoidance and denial is to never be fully alive, to truly *feel.*

The emotional and mental splitting from your body that formerly meant your survival during the abuse is now backfiring. Your perpetual state of slumber has become a waking nightmare. Your real self is hidden, out of reach. You are out of contact with your own body. In order to recover, you will have to re-learn to integrate your body with your mind, and your emotions with your thoughts. Emotions are not just states of mind, they are also states of body.

As a victim, you may be so emotionally and psychologically cut off from your body that you literally do not know how you feel at any given time. Usually you try to *think* about how you are feeling. As an alternative to that, try to start paying attention to how your body expresses emotion. Our bodies experience a different set of physical sensations for each emotion. When we feel *angry,* our muscles become tense, anticipating action. When we feel *sad,* our throats become constricted, our eyes begin to water. *Fear* can cause us to lift up our shoulders, cover up our stomachs, and stiffen our bodies. We each have our own ways of physically expressing how we feel. Begin to notice your body signals, and you will learn to differentiate one feeling response from another.

We also need to change our *beliefs* about feelings. There is no "positive" or "negative" feeling. *All* feelings are natural and good. We need to learn that anger is not a negative emotion. It is what we *do* with it that makes it constructive or destructive. If we repress it or turn it against ourselves, it becomes destructive. If we take it out on someone who doesn't deserve it, it has served no good purpose. But if we vent it in a positive way, such as talking it out with the person we are angry with or beating a pillow, it becomes constructive. We also need to realize that our feelings will not perpetuate themselves forever. We may fear that if we start crying we will never stop. But we will cry only as long as there are tears to be shed, as long as it takes to reach a sense of completion, however partial. We may be afraid that if we get angry there will be no end to it. But we will be angry only as long as there is anger to be expressed.

If we want to be fully alive—able to love and enjoy other people, share our thoughts and feelings with friends and loved ones, break out of our isolation—then we must be willing to take the risk and allow ourselves to feel and express all our emotions.

YOUR INNER CHILD

When you were a child you were in touch with your emotions far more than you are now as an adult. In order to reconnect with emotions you long ago cut off, it will be necessary for you to reach inside yourself to reconnect with your inner child. Most of us forget the small child that is a part of us, the child we were, with her fears, insecurities, and desperate need to be loved. But within all of us, this inner child still exists.

In order to heal the wounds of our past we must love, comfort, and nurture the little child within us. Get to know your inner child. Learn to treat her as a good parent would a cherished son or daughter. Listen to her needs. Your inner child needs to learn to trust that *you* (the *adult* part of you) will not be neglectful and abusive like the other adults in her life have been. Unfortunately, we often end up perpetuating the cycle by being as neglectful and abusive toward our inner child as our parents were toward us. We ignore our child; we are ashamed of her, we do not take care of her in appropriate ways. We pretend that her feelings of fear and insecurity and her need to be loved do not exist.

Start by remembering what kind of a child you were. Close your eyes and visualize your child at a time when she was very much in need of nurturing and protection. Take in the entire image, including facial expression and body posture. You may see yourself as a baby, a toddler, or an older child—the image is significant, since it may represent when you were most in need. Accept this inner child, who has been emotionally starved and had to pretend that feelings did not exist. Don't continue depriving her of the love and support she so urgently cries out for.

A good way to identify and care for your inner child is to buy a stuffed animal or doll for her. Do you remember the wonderful warmth and security you felt by holding your special childhood toy? Your inner child needs that comfort once again. Take your inner child to a store and spend lots of time choosing just the right stuffed animal or doll for her recovery process. Many people resist the idea of getting a stuffed animal—it's "silly" and "childish," and hugging an animal seems embarrassing. But most of my clients get past this quickly, once they let themselves feel the comfort it brings and realize the extent to which the child in them needs nurturing.

Stacey was one of them: "When we first talked about a stuffed animal I thought the idea was ridiculous. But one day while shopping I noticed the most darling stuffed dog. I couldn't resist picking it up. All of a sudden I found myself having feelings of *love* for it. Now when I feel afraid or alone I hug my dog, and I don't feel so bad." Similarly, Barbara resisted buying a toy for some time, but finally gave in. Much to her surprise, and even though she does not fully understand why, she feels comforted by it. She confided, "Last night I searched desperately for my bear before I went to bed."

Another way to acknowledge and nurture your inner child is to have a dialogue with her. This can be a verbal or written dialogue, an imaginary conversation between the adult part of you and the child part of you. Start your dialogue with a question like "How are you today?" or "What's the matter?" or "You seem upset, is something bothering you?" With practice, your inner child will express what she is feeling. The adult will then be able to listen to the child, soothe her, and become her "good" parent.

While you work on each step of your recovery program, continue your dialogue with your inner child. Check with her often to see how she feels. Listen to her closely. She will tell you what you need in order to feel safer and more secure. She will also tell you when you are neglecting her (your emotional needs). If you give her what she needs, you will be better able to continue in your recovery process to completion.

CHAPTER 4

Hope for Recovery

IF YOU WERE a victim of childhood sexual abuse, you will be relieved to know that now *there is hope for recovery.* Of course, nothing can change the past; what happened to you happened. But what you *can* change is how you feel about the past. You can put a stop to the way your past has been crippling you in the present.

Through greater social awareness you will now be among the first generation of people to have the opportunity to recover from the devastation of childhood sexual abuse. The chances are high that your parents, grandparents, and great-grandparents were also sexually abused, but at a time when society was not ready to examine the problem. For them, there was little hope. Unrecovered, they took their anger, pain, and frustration out on you and other children. And this is why the cycle of abuse has continued up to the present day. Today, however, people all over the country are recovering from the damage caused by such abuse. Hundreds of support groups exist, and many therapists now understand and are better trained to handle the special needs of sex-abuse victims.

Having been a victim does not mean you will remain a victim. You can become a survivor, and eventually you can recover. Thousands of people have overcome the effects of such abuse and are happier, healthier, and more well-adjusted; no longer ruled by pain and suffering, they are now able to love freely and have found sexual fulfillment.

What does recovery mean? It means to improve, to regain, to get well, to *heal.* It is within your reach to improve the quality of your life substantially, to increase your sense of self-worth, to regain your lost pride, and to heal the wounds of childhood sexual abuse.

THE RECOVERY PROCESS

When I first started working with childhood sexual abuse victims, I noticed that each person seemed to go through a similar process in working toward recovery. From this awareness I developed the seven steps to recovery.

The recovery process developed in this book includes those seven steps, which are: (1) facing the truth; (2) releasing your anger; (3) confronting with the facts and with your feelings; (4) resolving your relationships; (5) rediscovering yourself; (6) self-care; (7) forgiving yourself.

Facing the truth. To free yourself from the past, first you must face the truth about what really happened. Some victims don't even remember what happened to them; their unconscious has been shielding them from the truth. Other victims do indeed remember, but have never fully faced the truth and allowed themselves to feel their pain. Aware or not, the abuse will continue to run your life until you come to terms with it. Only then can the pain be overcome and the victim emerge a freer human being.

Releasing your anger. Once you have faced the truth, you will become more aware of the tremendous amount of anger you feel toward the perpetrator and those who did not protect you. You are entitled to be angry at all those who contributed to your abuse. You will learn to release this anger in constructive ways that will not add to your difficulties but will instead give you more strength and vitality.

Confronting with facts and feelings. After you have constructively released your anger, you will feel strong enough to confront those who have hurt you. In order to regain your personal power so that you will not continue to be a victim, you will need to confront the important people in your life—parents, the perpetrator, and other members of your family—either directly or indirectly. By confronting with facts and feelings you will pave the way for a possible reconciliation with those who have hurt, neglected, and abused you. At the very least, confronting will bring closure to those relationships that plague you the most.

Resolving your relationships. Your recovery process is going to change you, your relationships, and how you view those relationships. Once you have faced the truth and begun releasing your anger, you will be able to look at your relationships more objectively. You may choose to temporarily separate from, divorce from, or reconcile with significant people from your past. You will learn to determine which relationships are healthy and which are unhealthy. At this point you will be strong enough to disconnect from those relationships that are unhealthy, abusive, or that hold no promise of improvement.

Rediscovering yourself. Childhood sexual abuse inhibits the development of a sense of self that is separate from your parents, your relatives, and the person who abused you. Within you is a person who is a unique combination of all your experiences, feelings, thoughts, and sensations. You are now ready to increase your self-awareness and your self-knowledge. You are about to journey into your mind, your emotions, and your sensations on the most exciting adventure in your life.

Self-care. Once you have rediscovered your *self,* you will need to learn how to take care of that self. Those who were sexually abused as children most likely came from dysfunctional families that rarely conveyed how to take care of oneself properly. Instead, they were taught to focus on the needs of others. You will begin to learn to put your own needs first when appropriate, to ask for what you want, and to say no to what you don't want. In addition, it will be important to give yourself what you missed as a child and to value, respect, nurture, and love yourself.

Forgiving yourself. When you realize how and why you have treated yourself poorly in the past, you will understand the necessity of learning to forgive yourself. You have spent a lot of time feeling guilty for the abuse and for the things you have done as a consequence of the abuse, both as a child and as an adult. You will need to free yourself of this guilt by learning to differentiate between those actions you are responsible for and those you are not. For those actions you truly are responsible for (abusing your own children, for example) you will need to make amends. But for those actions you are not responsible for (your own sexual abuse), you will need to forgive yourself—*and* your body.

HOW LONG DOES RECOVERY TAKE?

Recovery takes patience, perseverance, and good old-fashioned guts. At least two or three years are usually required. Remember, what happened to you was devastating. You must give yourself time to heal. You might say, "Two or three years! I'll be almost middle-aged when I finish the recovery process." To that I can only ask, "Where will you be in two or three years if you *don't* work toward recovery?"

The amount of time it will take for you to recover will depend on a number of factors: (1) the severity and duration of the abuse; (2) the amount of openness and honesty you are able to develop about the abuse; (3) the amount of support you receive from family and friends, a therapist, or a support group; and (4) the amount of time you spend working on recovery, not just in therapy or in your support group but outside of these as well. Clients who recovered most quickly were those who spent time each day writing about their feelings and allowing themselves to release their emotions in constructive ways.

For some people, the process may take even longer than two or three years. Although everyone suffers a betrayal of trust, whether they were fondled or raped, there are nevertheless factors that determine how much damage there may be and how long a recovery period is necessary. Victims who were continually abused over a number of years or were abused by more than one perpetrator seem to need the longest recovery time.

In any case, be patient. Find your own pace so that you can progress at the rate most natural for you. If you start pushing yourself before you are ready or become critical of yourself for not progressing faster, you will only prolong your period of recovery.

HOW WILL YOU KNOW YOU HAVE RECOVERED?

You will not suddenly wake up one morning to find that it's all better, all solved, all symptoms miraculously disappeared. Recovery is a *process,* and as such, evidence of your having changed will come gradually and slowly. At first you may not even recognize how much you have recovered because the changes may be so subtle. The recovery process is full of ups and downs. There will be times when you will feel incredibly good, better than you have felt in your life. The dark cloud that has hung over you will have lifted, and you will begin to feel some joy instead of continual pain.

But remember that feelings often come in layers. Once a layer of anger has been released you will be confronted with the pain that is just underneath. At these times you may feel like you are backsliding. You aren't. You are getting better. In actuality, you have gained the strength necessary to face deeper, even more painful feelings and awarenesses.

A client described this process: "I start to feel great for a while and think I have reached recovery, and then another memory washes over me and I come crashing down. I realize there is yet another incidence of abuse, another issue I must deal with, or deeper feelings to release. But then I try to approach recovery in another way, as if I were walking up a long series of staircases. After climbing up mile after mile, I finally, ecstatically, reach what I think is the top, only to look up and discover I have only reached a landing. It's devastating. But then I start to appreciate the landing. I can look down and see how far I've come. I can rest and regain the strength to go on. Then, when I'm ready, I can continue up. Is there a top at all? Who cares? Each landing is a triumph in itself."

As you continue your journey you will come to realize that there are no roads that guarantee a safe arrival. You will have as your constant companions both risk and the joy of discovery. Your destination will continually change; as soon as you have arrived at one, you will become anxious to set out for the next. Savor the excitement of your journey; in it you will receive your greatest rewards.

WHAT ARE THE SPECIFIC BENEFITS OF RECOVERY?

Higher self-esteem. You will begin to feel significantly better about yourself. Since you will actually start *liking* yourself, perhaps for the first time, you will take better care of yourself—physically, emotionally, and spiritually. You may finally be able to lose or gain weight, stop or cut down on your alcohol, smoking, or drug use, and end other forms of self-destructive behavior. As you grow to love yourself and your body more, you will be less and less willing to abuse it.

Improved relationships. You will know that you deserve to be treated with caring and respect, and you will no longer accept abusive treatment from others. You will realize that you don't have to be either a victim or a victimizer. You will feel more equal to others; you should no longer feel the need to please them or control them. You will replace your unhealthy relationships with healthy ones. This newfound love for yourself will set you free to love others, and your similarly newfound trust will encourage new, meaningful friendships.

You can also look forward to a time when you will be able to have close, intimate relationships. Instead of going from one relationship to the next, you will be able to maintain long-lasting ties that are healthy and fulfilling. If you are in an unhealthy relationship now, you will develop the strength and self-confidence to end it. If you have felt isolated to the point where you are unable to have close relationships at all, you will begin to feel safe enough to reach out to others.

Improved sexuality. Since most of your sexual problems were caused by unresolved feelings concerning the sexual abuse, you have reason to expect considerable improvement in this area. Recovery unlocks your natural desire and ability to enjoy your sexuality, perhaps for the first time. Flashbacks that have kept you plagued by the past subside or disappear entirely, enabling you to stay present during sex. You will be able to experience feelings of your *own* choice as you once again have control over your body. As you stop linking sex with power or anger, or love with pain, you will be able to relinquish the unhealthy sexual associations for positive ones, connecting sex with love, and love with pleasure.

Increased ability to understand, express, and release your emotions. Your emotions are the key to your recovery. As you get to know yourself through your emotions, you will feel far less confused and overwhelmed by your reactions. Only by expressing your pain, anger, and fear concerning the sexual abuse can you truly put the past aside. You will be relieved of depression, nightmares, phobias, obsessive thoughts and behavior, and flashbacks. Your anger will subside and with it your uncontrollable outbursts and abusive behavior toward yourself and others.

Relief from physical symptoms. As you release the past through your emotions, so will you be able to release the memories of the abuse still held in your body. Such physical reminders as frequent sore throats, difficulty swallowing, or vaginal or anal pain will disappear, and many of your muscular aches and pains will subside as the tension created by holding in these emotions is released. In addition, you will find that you will stop hurting yourself "accidentally," as your self-hate is turned into healthy anger toward the abuser.

Greater sense of control. In addition to the above benefits, you can look forward to feeling more in control of your life. You will be able to go about the business of everyday living—taking care of your body, your finances, your clothes, your car. Most important, you will feel less helpless and dependent on others for support and survival.

For most of the time Janet was in therapy, she felt so out of control of her emotions that she could hardly keep her life together. Overwhelmed by feelings of anger and pain, she had a difficult time concentrating and couldn't hold down a job. Like many survivors, she felt particularly out of control while working on the abuse, during which time she was bringing up old memories and releasing repressed long-buried emotions. But as she reached recovery, she began to feel more capable, competent, and in charge of herself: "Life doesn't seem so hard now. I go about my daily routine with far less stress. My house is clean, my checkbook is balanced, and I have a great job!"

Feeling more in control of your life and your feelings also extends to feeling less fearful of being out of control with food, alcohol, sex, and other potential addictions. Your increased control with other people means you are less likely to allow others to control you, and less inclined to need to control others.

Greater self-control will also enable you to avoid sabotaging yourself and your recovery. For example, you will no longer need to stay in negative, destructive relationships to punish yourself or because you feel you deserve to be treated badly. Now you know that a good relationship is your right. As Chris confided to me, "It used to be that when men treated me well I felt uncomfortable, like I didn't deserve it.

I would tell myself they were wimps and would seek out more neglectful, abusive men instead. Now, even though I still feel uncomfortable when someone is nice to me, I don't sabotage the relationship by being cruel to them. I just tell myself, 'You deserve to be treated nicely,' and try to take it in."

Heightened self-awareness. Another way that you will feel more in control as you recover is that you will begin living more consciously. Freed from the "fog" of your pain, fear, and confusion, you will awaken and see the world revealed as never before. You will begin to *observe* things, especially yourself. You will begin to be aware of what you do and *why* you do it. You will begin to observe your own behavior and attitudes. This will enable you to begin consciously working on changing your bad habits and self-defeating behaviors.

Lucy came to her session one day full of excitement about a recent discovery: "I've started noticing how very critical I tend to be. The other night, as I drove my car into the driveway, I got furious because there were toys all over the yard and my oldest son had not taken the garbage cans back in. In my mind I started berating the kids: 'These kids don't appreciate what I do for them. I work all day and come home tired, and they can't even help out!' I couldn't believe what was going through my mind! It was more habit than anything else—I didn't even feel that angry at them. Then I realized that I sounded just like my father when he would come home from work. And in the past, I would have acted just like him as well; I would have gone into the house yelling and screaming, berating each child for being a bad person and not ever appreciating anything I do, and upsetting everyone for the entire evening!"

Mary also benefited greatly from self-observation. She had been overweight for a long time. But while working through the sex-abuse issues, she had not attempted to lose weight.

She had told me, "I can handle just one thing at a time. I think I especially need food now, because it is the only thing that comforts me with all this pain." I supported her decision, believing that when she no longer needed this crutch, she would lose the weight.

One day, after Mary had been in therapy for a little over two years, she came to her session looking happier than I had ever seen her. "I had resigned myself," she said, "to thinking that I would always be fat. I figured I just didn't have the willpower or the motivation. Then last week, when I was driving home after our session, I got my usual urge to get some junk food. But this time, instead of heading for the nearest Burger King, I thought to myself, 'Why are you doing this? You'll just feel bad about yourself afterward. You just paid good money to see a therapist so that you could feel *better* about yourself, and now you are going to do this?

"Then I thought about why I always felt hungry when I left your office and realized it was because I felt *lonely* after I left you. You are the only person I have in my life who cares about me, so when I leave you I feel all alone and empty. I want to eat to get comfort and fill the emptiness. All week long I've watched when it is I feel hungry, and often it is when I feel lonely. So I started trying to just feel that feeling when it happened and hugged my bear, or else I phoned someone. A couple of times I ate anyway, but at least I knew why. I feel so great! Now I don't feel so wildly out of control all the time. I guess I'm getting better, huh?"

Indeed, Mary was getting better. She was learning to live her life more consciously.

Staying grounded in the present. Prior to recovery you may be suffering from recurrent and intrusive recollections of past traumatic events. There were many times when you suddenly began acting or feeling as if the traumatic event were recurring. Often a person, a place, or a feeling would trigger memories and suddenly take you back in time. And, often, because you were unaware that this process was actually going on, you may have confused the past with the present. A definite sign of recovery is when you can distinguish the past from the present even when you are exposed to events or people who symbolize or resemble past traumatic events.

Once you are firmly headed toward recovery, you will be able to stay grounded in the present and not allow memories from the past to control you. Peggy, who had been in therapy for three years and was making remarkable headway, related this story: "I've been getting really angry at my tennis instructor. He's teaching us in a group how to serve, and he lines us up and then goes down the line to check on us. Last week he just passed right by me and went on to concentrate on the others. This really upset me. After all, I paid my money just like the others did. I tried to tell myself that he passed me up because I'm doing so well, but I still wanted some attention. Finally, I just got so angry that I walked off the courts.

"When I got home I was still furious. So I got out my plastic bat and beat my bed. Afterward, I started to cry. I realized why I had been so angry and hurt. The tennis instructor reminded me of my mother, who never took any time to be with me. I was reminded of how I had felt ignored and invisible around my parents. Now I felt invisible to that instructor! I was able to go back the next week and tell him that I wanted him to make sure he spent some time with me this lesson. I wasn't going to be invisible anymore!"

Peggy realized that the reason she reacted so strongly was that the situation reminded her of something from the past. Now that she was more in control of her life, she was not allowing her past to run her life.

Another client, Cindy, shared her experience of being able to differentiate present events from those in the past: "Now I know what it feels like to experience something that ordinarily would have taken me back to the past, but to realize *while it is happening* that the past isn't happening again now. I was at the dentist, and he asked me to open my mouth. I could feel my jaw getting tight as it usually does, and I started resisting. Then I suddenly realized: This is the *dentist.* He isn't going to hurt you—he's just trying to help you have better teeth."

Even though the experience of being with a man and opening her mouth triggered a *body memory* in Cindy and catapulted her back to the times when her stepfather would force her to perform fellatio on him, she was now able to realize that it *wasn't* the same thing, it *wasn't* happening again. She could now differentiate the past from the present.

Although you may always overreact *initially* to a situation that triggers a memory, as you get healthier you will discover *why* you are reacting, what the trigger is, and what it reminds you of, and you'll realize it isn't happening in the present. There will always be people who will remind you of the perpetrator or your parents or anyone else who hurt you, but you will be able to recognize people as their own unique selves instead of mere shadows from your past.

Developing healthier defenses. Another benefit of recovery is the fact that you will be able to let go of many behaviors that have been holding you back from living a freer, more peaceful life. For example, you developed survival skills that helped you to survive all the neglect, deprivation, and abuse of your childhood. But you will discover that these survival skills are no longer needed. You are no longer a child; you have more power now. You are no longer in danger. Although splitting off from yourself and disconnecting from your feelings helped you to survive the abuse of your childhood, these defense mechanisms can prevent you from experiencing life's joys as well as its pains, and they can get in your way of having close, intimate relationships with others.

Self-discovery. In addition to relinquishing some of your defenses, you will also find yourself letting go of many of your negative beliefs. You will discover that many of the so-called truths you were raised with and forced to believe are not truths at all. With this perspective, you will come to see, for example, that the names you were called as a child are simply not true—you are *not* "stupid," "lazy," "ugly," or a "liar."

As you begin to let go of the negative, false beliefs about yourself, you can discover just who you really are. You can let go of your pretenses and masks and discover who the real person is underneath. As Jeri said, "I was everybody else. I was always doing what someone else wanted me to do, not what I wanted to do. I didn't even *know* what I wanted to do or who I was. I was like a chameleon, with other people's thoughts and beliefs making up the façade of 'Jeri.' Now I am learning what *I* want, how *I* feel, what *I* believe—and it feels great."

Vicki was also very pleased when she started learning who she was. "I always put up this pretense of being really strong. I was always there for everyone else, always the one who could be calm in a crisis. But I discovered that I was really scared and vulnerable underneath. My role as caretaker was just my way of hiding pain and fear. It was hard facing that. I hated what I saw. But I am glad now that I was finally honest with myself. Now I can be strong and vulnerable both. That feels good. It feels more real."

Ron was relieved to discover there even *was* a real person underneath the false image of himself that he had worked hard to develop for years. "I was so certain that when my defenses came down there would be nothing left of me. That wall I put up when I was very young was so strong I believed that when it came down so would I. Well, I surprised myself. There *was* something behind the wall, I'm still here, and I can feel! Not a lot yet, mind you, but I'm just beginning."

Along with your false self-image, your false illusions will

also tumble, the most significant of which is the illusion of being in control of what you cannot control. When the abuse was occurring you probably fooled yourself into believing that you had control, an illusion that was vital to your survival. But today it is getting in your way. You need to sit back, and, bit by bit, feel how helpless, innocent, and out of control you were. Only by acknowledging the fact that you were truly out of control and that you were a *victim* will you be able to stop being a victim *now.* The only person you need to be in control of is yourself.

Greater peace of mind. As you recover, you will develop a more realistic view of the future. You will stop setting yourself up for disappointment after disappointment by having unrealistic fantasies of "how things will be." Instead of false hopes and unreasonable expectations, you will learn to set realistic goals for yourself, including your progress toward recovery. You will begin to let go of your attraction (or addiction) to chaos as you realize that there is excitement in just living your life in a healthy, realistic, peaceful way. Because your entire childhood may have been riddled with one crisis after another, you grew accustomed to this level of intensity.

As you reach recovery, your life will begin to be less chaotic. You will find there are times when you actually feel happy and calm. Many survivors initially experience these times as confusing or upsetting. "It's as if I keep waiting for the other shoe to drop," one client related. "I can't believe things are going so well, so I assume there is trouble just around the corner." Others actually experience these times as boring. "My life is getting too predictable. I feel happier and calmer, but there's no excitement. I actually catch myself wanting to call my parents or my ex-husband, just to stir things up a little."

MAKING YOUR COMMITMENT

By now it should be clear: *recovery is possible.* A new life is possible. But neither is possible without a commitment to begin and complete the journey. *It's the single most important thing you can do to assure your recovery.* A commitment is your promise to yourself to go through all the steps required in the recovery process and to stick with it, no matter what. The agreement is *not* "I will work through the trauma of the abuse *if* I can." And it is also not "I'll do it unless it gets too painful." It is saying with conviction, "I will continue working through the effects of the abuse until I reach recovery." This commitment will keep you going through the rough spots, when your resistance to change will be the strongest. Think of this commitment as a symbol of your dedication to recovery. You have made the choice to recover because you want to improve the quality of your life. Remember: *Recovery is the positive choice. The alternative is to continue suffering.*

Some of you may find that making a commitment is difficult, since in the past, "commitments" you made or felt may have trapped you in the abusive situation, or suffocated you with the abuser's demands. They may have felt like obligations and duties. Your commitment to your childhood family may have even contributed to your abuse, since you may have felt obligated to keep the family together.

But this promise you make to yourself to recover is different from previous commitments. No one is going to force you to work through your problems. You are the person who decides to solve your problems because you want a better life than the one you are experiencing now.

Some survivors get angry at having to work at recovering from sexual abuse. They feel that it is unfair. They suffered all their life because of what someone else did to them; why should they have to suffer even more pain? This anger at "having" to do something is similar to the anger they felt at "having" to put up with someone's sexual advances and demands, or "having" to perform sexually. Now, whenever they feel like they don't have a choice, they get angry, resistant, and afraid.

Well, this is different. You do not "have to" work on your problems or go to therapy or join a support group. But rest assured: Choosing to continue the way you have been would be like choosing slavery over freedom.

If you do choose to make a commitment to your recovery, there will still be times when you may want to revert to your former ways of dealing with the experience of having been abused. You may make up excuses as to why you cannot go to your therapist, participate in your group meeting, or take the next action necessary for recovery, particularly when you are dealing with something especially painful. As you know, ignoring the pain and denying the reality of the experience simply doesn't work. You need to commit to a more active mode, a path that takes you through your pain and out the other side to recovery.

Your friends and family may become frightened or discouraged because they will see your anger and sadness more clearly than they see your progress. Some may have little understanding of what you are undergoing. Explain the recovery process to them. Ask them to read this book. Do not let their misgivings discourage you. Instead, tell them about your commitment to recovery. Even if these do not satisfy their needs, it will reinforce your own sense of commitment.

Some of the seven recovery steps may seem easier or more difficult than others. Neither ease nor difficulty should impede your progress. If the step is easy, you can increase your pace. If the step is difficult, you can slow your pace. You are in charge.

A technique to reinforce your commitment to recovery is to list all the reasons why you want to recover.

My Commitment to Recovery

I want to recover because

1. __________
2. __________
3. __________
4. __________
5. __________
6. __________
7. __________
8. __________
9. __________
10. __________

You may be able to think of many more reasons. List them all. They mark the beginning of your recovery. Review your list periodically. It will serve as a reminder of how important your recovery is to you.

Here is what some of my clients had to say about their recovery process. Perhaps these words will encourage you.

> "My entire life has improved because of the work I have done in my recovery process. I am no longer promiscuous, and I quit drugs. For the first time in my life I like myself!"

> "I now feel like pursuing my dreams and goals. Before, I was so caught up in healing myself from the past that I couldn't even imagine a future! I don't sabotage my success like I used to, and now I complete those things I set out to do."

> "I joined a support group because I had started physically abusing my son. I wanted to make certain that I would not continue the cycle of violence. That goal kept me going through the rough spots."

"My life could only get better. I had reached bottom. Even though I felt pain during recovery, it wasn't anything like the pain I suffered every day before I started therapy."

"Working toward recovery gave me the hope of being able to be in charge of my life instead of continuing to be a victim of my past."

"I didn't even know I had been sexually abused when I first started therapy, but finding out explained so much of my behavior to myself. Even though the recovery process was often difficult, the more I understood myself, the more encouraged I felt. It feels so wonderful to no longer be a mystery to myself."

"I knew that working through the abuse was the only way I was going to survive. Recovery was my last hope, otherwise I knew I would kill myself—either by suicide or with drugs and alcohol."

You can learn to make the rest of your life the best of your life. Making a genuine commitment marks the start of the best part of your life, a time when you can begin to look forward instead of looking back. You cannot look forward to a life completely *free* of pain (no one can), but to a life free of *continual* pain. You cannot look forward to a life *free* of problems, but to a life filled with the courage to face whatever problems come your way. And most important, you will feel good about yourself. You can face the world with a sense of hope, a determination to make the rest of your life the best it can be.

As someone who has endured the trauma of childhood sexual abuse, you've already been through the worst. Draw upon the inner strength that enabled you to survive. Your life can only get better. Don't let anything or anyone—including yourself—stop you from reaching recovery.

PART II

Your Journey To Recovery

STEP 1

Facing the Truth

THE TRUTH ABOUT your own sexual abuse has probably been obscured for years by layers of denial and deceit. Now you must begin to peel away those painful layers. Protecting yourself and others from the truth will only impede your progress. While in the past you avoided the pain by blocking out the sexual abuse altogether, you now must face the abuse bit by bit, layer by layer, until the truth is told.

The perpetual lies and deceptions have kept you confused, distorting your reality and causing you to blame and doubt yourself. Facing the truth will enable you to regain your sense of innocence and place the blame where it belongs. The truth may hurt, but it cannot harm you. Knowing the truth is vitally important to reversing the damage you have experienced.

You know the pain of living with lies. Now, in order to free yourself from the pain and scars of the abuse, it is important to recall forgotten memories, to stop denying and minimizing the abuse, and to stop defending your family and the abuser. Stop lying to others, and stop lying to yourself. You will face many truths in the recovery process: truths about what really happened, truths about your parents and the rest of your childhood family, truths about the abuser, and finally truths about yourself.

Your family will not appreciate your inquiries about the abuse. They may even try to discourage you. But in choosing to continue to face the real truth about your sexual abuse, you are consciously choosing to become a survivor rather than remain a victim. The truth will not come all at once but will unfold layer by layer. Each time you face one truth about what really happened, another will reveal itself. Face each truth as it surfaces.

START TELLING THE TRUTH

Start by telling *yourself* the truth about the sexual abuse you experienced. For a long time you have tried to fool yourself by whitewashing what happened—by telling yourself it wasn't so bad. Admit to yourself that it *was* so bad; it was horrible enough to have affected your entire life. Call the trauma by its real name: sexual abuse, sexual assault, rape, incest, or molestation. You weren't "having an affair," or "having sex" with the abuser, and he was not "caressing you" or "making love to you."

Encourage yourself to tell the truth by starting a "truth book." Write down all the details of the abuse: when it happened, where it happened, who did it, exactly how it was done, how many times it was done, how it felt, how you feel about it now, and how it affects your life. Make a commitment to yourself to write down only the truth—not the way you *wish* things were, but the way things really were and the way you really feel about it. Getting your story down in black and white is a permanent testament to your pain, betrayal, and eventually to your survival and recovery. If trying to write the truth doesn't work for you, use a tape recorder.

Eventually, you will tell the truth to your support group, your therapist, or to a trusted friend or family member. Break the silence that has been suffocating you. When the truth remains hidden, it smothers us. You have been living in a world of secrecy, isolated from everyone, even your closest family and friends. The only way to break through the silence, secrecy, and ensuing isolation is to *start telling the truth.*

REMEMBERING THE TRUTH

Why Is It So Important to Remember?

When you were abused, those around you acted as if it weren't happening. Since no one else acknowledged the abuse, you sometimes felt that it wasn't real. Because of this you felt confused. You couldn't trust your own experience and perceptions. Moreover, others' denial led you to suppress your memories, thus further obscuring the issue.

You can end your own denial by remembering. Allowing yourself to remember is a way of confirming in your own mind that you didn't just imagine it. Because the person who abused you did not acknowledge your pain, you may have also thought that perhaps it wasn't as bad as you felt it was. In order to acknowledge to yourself that it really was that bad, you need to remember as much detail as possible. Because by denying what happened to you, you are doing to yourself exactly what others have done to you in the past: You are negating and denying yourself.

As a result of your attempts to block out fear and pain, you have blocked out the good along with the bad. Days, months, or years of your childhood may be erased from your memory. It is as if you did not exist during that time. But you did exist. You went to school, made friends, and played games. Remembering the painful times will help you recapture those forgotten moments and reclaim your childhood.

Ways to Remember

You can examine all the memorabilia of your childhood—photographs, report cards, artwork, school projects. These items will tell your story, even if you don't remember. If you are in therapy or in a support group, bring in your memorabilia, especially your photos, so that others can see them. Other victims are the best people to get feedback from, since they can spot childhood sexual abuse faster than anyone else. You may discover, for instance, a set of photos showing a change in you from an open-faced, smiling child to a sullen or expressionless, withdrawn one. Such a visible change is a clue that you probably suffered some significant psychological trauma. Determining as precisely as possible when the contrasting photos were taken will tell you the time frame in which the abuse began. Photos of homes in which you lived may further jog your memory. Another clue may be found in photographs of you standing or sitting apart from the rest of the family; such photographs frequently show the alienation you experienced in the family. Or, if the abuser was a member or close associate of the family, you may find him positioned close to you in a photograph. Often, snapshots unmask the incestuous relationship rather obviously. One client found the first clue to her long-buried incestuous relationship with her father revealed most blatantly. In a photograph of her father holding her on his knees, her legs are spread wide open and his hand is up her dress. Another survivor can be seen at fourteen in a family photo picturing her father standing next to her with his arm around her. At first glance there is nothing unusual, but closer examination reveals his arm around her shoulder and his hand right on her breast.

Other survivors have found more than clues. They have unearthed startling evidence, sometimes in the form of nude photographs of themselves that the perpetrator had taken. Far from being cute naked-baby-on-the-bearskin-rug photos, these document children posed in sexually provocative positions.

By recognizing these blatant indicators of abuse, which they may have seen before but not identified, most victims are appalled. Others, still in denial, actually have trouble identifying the sexuality that is obvious to others. This is another reason to share your photos with those you trust or with your therapy group. It may take feedback from others for you to clearly see what the photos are depicting.

Clues can be found as well in other childhood memorabilia. Report cards offer a rich source of data. A sudden drop in your grades, for instance, may reflect the devastating impact the abuse had on you and may pinpoint the onset of the abuse. Additionally, report cards often contain valuable feedback from teachers. Survivors are amazed to read such messages sent home by teachers as: "Mary is not able to concentrate on her schoolwork. She daydreams a lot and pulls at her hair." One teacher even inquired, "Linda's schoolwork has dropped off so drastically this semester. Is she having trouble at home?" Of course, sometimes photos and report cards reveal little or nothing, since you may have become a high achiever to compensate for your pain or may have learned very early on to put on a happy face and hide your feelings from the world.

Artwork can also provide clues, since children often express their true feelings in their art. One client brought me several pictures she had painted as a child that clearly revealed that she was being sexually abused. One picture depicted a little girl with a large wound in her torso; another was of a "monster" with a huge penis; a third pictured her house, with her bedroom dark and foreboding.

Dreams can also be very revealing, exposing memories you have been unwilling or unable to face during waking hours. Judy, for instance, who had known that her brother had sexually abused her, dreamt that her father also molested her. She awoke to a terrible pain in her vagina and a flood of memories. Indeed, she realized, the dream was true.

Keep a writing pad and a pen beside your bed. When you awaken, immediately write down whatever dreams or fragments of dreams you remember. They can be a valuable source of clues. Nightmares should also be recorded, even though they are frightening and debilitating. If you don't remember all the details, write down how the dream made you feel. This can be important in understanding other dreams, recalling forgotten memories, and accepting more of your own feelings.

Why Is It So Difficult to Remember?

Sexually abused children are subjected to high degrees of physical and emotional stress. They are flooded with intense feelings of pain, fear, panic, anger, and betrayal—feelings they are emotionally unequipped to handle. Being forced to submit to the will of the abuser robs the child of any sense of control over her own experience. When no other help is available, victims frequently rely on indirect methods of coping. These methods of self-protection are called defense mechanisms.

The most common self-protection or defense mechanism is a process known as *dissociation,* in which victims "blank out" or mentally divorce themselves from their experience. Some victims dissociate by concentrating all their awareness on something else—a part of their own body that is not being invaded or sounds outside the room. This intense concentration can take them completely away from the horrifying experience at hand. Melissa, who was repeatedly forced to submit to her father's sexual touches, told her group how she would focus all her attention on looking for a certain spot on the ceiling: "This would take a lot of concentration. Sometimes by the time I found the *exact* spot, it would be all over. It was as if it hadn't happened at all."

Similarly, others did what they now call "checking out" or "flying away," projecting their consciousness into an object or to another place. Jessica explained her process of dissociation to me as "going into the lamp overhead" while her uncle molested her. "I was no longer being pushed up against the wall. I was inside of the lamp, safe from harm."

Although these methods of self-protection help the victim survive the abuse, they can cause the victim to lose all memory of the experience or have only vague, dreamlike recall of it. This may then cause victims to end up believing that it may not have really happened at all.

Because of this kind of dissociation process, many victims are able to remember the abuse only when a certain object, smell, color, scene, or experience triggers a sudden, severe reaction. Lisa, who was having difficulty remembering the abuse she strongly suspected she had suffered, felt nausea and petrifying fear associated with the color blue. One day in therapy I asked her once again to close her eyes, take some deep breaths, and allow herself to try to remember the abuse. This particular day she immediately envisioned a patch of blue, and this time she understood, with terrifying clarity, what it meant. In between sobs, she told how her father had sodomized her while he held her head down against the carpet. "All I remembered about the abuse was the patch of blue in front of my face while he was assaulting me." Lisa's vivid recall was a milestone in her path toward recovery.

Understanding flashbacks. What Lisa experienced is called a *flashback*, an involuntary mental replay of a previous, vivid experience. During a flashback one seems to see, feel, hear, smell, or taste something from the past as if it were actually happening in the present. In a *visual* flashback, you actually *see* the scene of your abuse; or, as in Lisa's case, you may see a color, object, or image that reminds you or is symbolic of the abuse. In a *tactile* flashback, you actually *feel* sensations related to the abuse (vaginal, pelvic or anal pain, tingling, gagging, smothering, or the sensation of someone's hands on you) as if it were happening now. *Auditory* flashbacks include *hearing* someone breathe, cry, or snore as if they were present in the room you are occupying. Other victims have *olfactory* flashbacks, wherein they *smell* things associated with the abuse, such as after-shave. Whatever type of flashback you may have, you will feel as if you are being abused at that moment.

Many times, victims are caught completely off guard when they suddenly see, hear, taste, smell, or feel things for "no apparent reason." Some fear that they are going crazy. In fact, many seek therapy in the first place because they fear their flashback experience as a sign of mental illness. One in particular, Dana, came to me for therapy because she kept tasting semen in her mouth. No, she soon realized, she was not losing her mind, but instead was flashing back to the time when her uncle performed oral sex on her and ejaculated in her mouth.

In truth, flashbacks for most abuse victims are not signs of mental illness at all, but a normal response to having suffered a traumatic experience. Flashbacks are also common among Vietnam veterans, former POWs, hostages, survivors of terrorism, Holocaust survivors—anyone who suffers from what is called post-traumatic stress disorder.

Flashbacks are a clearing process of the mind. Like certain dreams, they provide a way for the mind to bypass both memory blocks and the defense mechanism of dissociation. Flashbacks are memories untouched by the passage of time. In the recovery process, a flashback can be an important part of remembering.

You cannot make yourself have a flashback, nor will you have one unless you are emotionally ready to remember something. Once remembered, the memory can help you to face more of the truth. You can then express your pent-up feelings about the memory and continue on your path to recovery. Think of the flashback as a clue to the next piece of work. No matter how painful, try to view it as a positive indication that you are now ready and willing to remember.

The Pain of Remembering

During this time of remembering you may often cry, feel angry, become frightened, feel out of control, or have difficulty dealing with others. You've hidden the truth from yourself for a long time, and now it will seem as if everything in your life needs to be questioned. Sometimes you may have difficulty just getting through the day. Realize that you are in the midst of a tremendous emotional upheaval. Be kind to yourself. The process of recovering from childhood sexual abuse is similar to that of recovering from a major surgery. You can't expect yourself to function at full capacity all at once. Take it easy and be patient.

You may feel particularly out of control as emotions you have buried emerge to the surface, threatening to overwhelm you. It may become difficult for you to go out of your house, to deal with people at work, or to be around your parents. Many victims go through a period of wanting to isolate themselves from others. These are all *normal* reactions, and they will pass. Your relationships may become strained as your anger surfaces. You may begin to take your anger out on those around you, those who do not deserve it. It is your responsibility to not confuse the past with the present. The next chapter discusses how to deal with the anger so you won't direct it toward family and friends with whom you are not really angry. Farther on, you will also get information on resolving relationships. Explain to your loved ones what you are going through, that you need their understanding. Ask them to read this book. This will give them a better understanding of you and will help them not to take your outbursts so personally.

Your sexuality may also be affected by the bad memories. You may have a difficult time making love with your partner because you feel sexually shut down. (It is common for survivors to lose all sexual feelings during parts of their recovery process.) You may be able to participate in only certain types of lovemaking, in certain positions and at specific times of the day. Or you may have flashbacks during sex. Once again, this too will pass. If you talk about all this to your partner, he or she will probably not take it personally and will be a support to you. (If your partner lacks any understanding of what is happening to you, you may need couples counseling.)

Truth Leads to Recovery

Most people who were sexually abused would just like to take a great big eraser and "make it all go away." Unfortunately, it will *not* go away, no matter what you try, and your attempts to deny it or forget it just prolong the pain. *Instead of trying to forget, try to remember.* If you spend the same amount of time remembering as you have spent trying to sweep it under the carpet, you will be a lot closer to recovery.

As Valerie recalled, "At first I could remember hardly anything about the abuse. All I knew was that it had happened and the way the room smelled, and so I built on that. The more I tried to remember, the more memories surfaced. When I could see the room in my mind's eye, I was finally able to remember what actually happened to me and how it felt."

The more Valerie remembered, the more pain she felt, and she had the natural tendency to try to block these memories. But as she continued to bring things out into the open, she felt herself moving more quickly toward recovery. "When I was able to *really* remember, I had a great sense of relief, even though I also felt sad and hurt. At least now I knew what I was dealing with. As difficult as it was on me to remember, it did give me back a part of my life that had become scary because it was so unknown and mysterious."

There is no need to push yourself. When you are emotionally strong enough to cope, more memories will return until you have looked the truth fully in the face. Therapy and support groups will give you the encouragement and support you need to keep up your courage.

As you do remember more and more about the abuse, you will need to face the truth about the perpetrator, your childhood family, and the abuse itself.

FACING THE TRUTH ABOUT THE PERPETRATOR

For most survivors, facing the truth about the perpetrator will be very difficult, because the chances are that the perpetrator was someone you knew well and was perhaps even in your family. If this is the case, you will probably have an emotional investment in protecting yourself from the truth.

As we have discussed in chapter 2, the majority of abusers are not strangers but in fact relatives, most notably stepfathers, fathers, uncles, brothers, and grandfathers. This explains why 85 percent of childhood sexual abuse occurs in the home.

If the perpetrator was one of your parents, facing the truth can be devastating. How can we acknowledge that our own parent, someone who was supposed to love and care for us, could care so little about us? What do we do with our feelings of love for them? We hate them for abusing us, for betraying us, for all the emotional harm they caused us, but we still love them.

Another reason for the difficulty in admitting the truth about the perpetrator, whether a parent or not, is the fact that he or she might have been among the few people in your life to give you any affection or attention. Since many victims of sexual abuse come from families in which there is little or no physical affection, the attention received from the perpetrator may have met such a strong emotional need that we cannot reconcile being angry with them, even though we know we "should be." If the perpetrator gave you the affection you longed for, allowing him to sexually fondle you may have seemed like a small price to pay. If he made you feel good about yourself in other ways, you will have a strong emotional investment in protecting your image of him.

Moreover, the perpetrator himself most likely went to lengths to deny, in one way or another, the nature of the abuse or even the abuse itself. But the truth is that no matter what the perpetrator had told you:

- He was *not* "teaching you" about sex or "preparing you for womanhood."
- He didn't "need" you or your body.
- It wasn't his "right."
- He wasn't making sure you wouldn't be cold like your mother.
- He wasn't "checking to make sure you were developing properly."
- He wasn't in love with you.
- He wasn't "too sick or too drunk to know what he was doing."

Further adding to your confusion about the truth is the fact that other family members may have also been "conned" by the perpetrator into believing what a "great guy" he is. If everyone around you sees the perpetrator as a loving, caring, generous person, how can you convince yourself, much less them, that he was a manipulative, cunning user of people? Cutting through the lies and denial about the perpetrator will be difficult, because so many family members continue to be deceived by him. Remember, they too have an investment in believing that he cares about them, that he is as he *appears* and not as he really is.

The *truth,* however, remains:

- He was using you to satisfy his own selfish needs.
- He was not considering your feelings or the effect it would have on you, and he didn't care about you enough to stop himself.
- He violated you and robbed you of your right to innocence.
- He forced his adult body onto or into your child's body.
- He betrayed your trust and in so doing caused you to be unable to trust others.
- He was responsible for his behavior, no matter how disturbed, alcoholic, or pathetic he seemed.
- He used his power, authority, and age to overpower you, threaten you, and instill in you a fear of others, of intimacy, of sex and sexual pleasure, and of yourself.
- He put an emotional wedge between you and your mother and the rest of your family.
- He made you feel "weird," "perverted," "different."

Face the truth. If you were strong enough to survive the abuse, you are strong enough to face it now.

FACING THE TRUTH ABOUT YOUR CHILDHOOD FAMILY

Although the responsibility for the sexual abuse itself is always the abuser's, families are often unwitting collaborators who can help "set the stage" for the abuse in a number of ways:

By denying you attention and affection. This made you vulnerable to someone who would exploit your needs.

By leaving you unsupervised—or poorly supervised—for lengthy periods of time. It takes time to molest a child. It takes time to prepare, coax, bribe; it takes time to earn trust. It takes time to get clothes off, touch, penetrate, ejaculate. Where were your parents or loving caretakers during all this time?

By leaving you with caretakers who were abusive, disturbed, or neglectful. Your family may have been unaware of or unwilling to see the caretaker's nature. They unwittingly contributed to your abuse each time they left you with that person. Some survivors even report that they were left with caretakers who were obviously alcoholic or emotionally disturbed and incapable of looking after children.

By abusing you physically, verbally, or emotionally. When your own parents don't value you, there is little possibility of you learning to value yourself. This makes it easier for a child molester to talk you into doing almost anything.

By ignoring obvious signs of abuse and cries for help. Parents of childhood sex-abuse victims are often so wrapped up in their own problems that they simply do not "see" their children at all. They may be protecting themselves from the awareness of their own childhood abuse. In addition, not "noticing" it protects them from having to take some action to stop it. A mother often does not notice the warning signs because she doesn't want to have to leave her husband. Grandparents have been known to "turn a blind eye" to abuse because they don't want to have to confront their son or daughter.

By making you feel they wouldn't believe you. You may have already related to your parents something that was true, only to be told that you were making it up or exaggerating.

As one woman put it, "I thought my mother would say it couldn't have happened, just like she had denied other things I had told her."

By showing other people they did not value you. This amounted to tacit permission for others to abuse you. Some parents have such disdain for their children that they believe they deserve to be mistreated and abused. One client, who was repeatedly sexually and physically abused by her baby-sitters said, "They saw how my mother felt about me, and so they treated me with disgust. If your own mother doesn't care about you, then why should others?"

By making you feel they couldn't or wouldn't protect you. Some adults feel as helpless and powerless as their children do, and therefore do not believe there is anything they can do about the abuse. If, for example, the women in your family felt powerless against the men, they probably not only allowed the men to do whatever they wanted to you, but they also taught you to feel powerless around men. If both your parents felt powerless when it came to *their* parents, they may have allowed your grandparents to molest you just as they may have been molested by them when they were children.

Childhood sexual abuse is an inherited disease. It is passed down from generation to generation. You are therefore probably not the only one in your family to have been molested. Your mother may have been victimized by her father, grandfather, uncle, or brother, and these men are likely to continue the cycle of abuse by molesting not only you but your siblings, cousins, nieces, and nephews. Your father may have been himself abused as a child or may have observed his father molesting another family member; this most likely perpetuated the cycle. Knowing these truths about your childhood family will help you resolve your relationships with them. Whether you tell the truth to any family member is up to you, but it is important to know the truth in order to make an informed choice.

FACING THE TRUTH ABOUT YOUR MOTHER

Most victims sooner or later have had to give up fantasies about their mothers: fantasies that she didn't know about the abuse, that she would have done something to stop it if she had known, fantasies of how much she cared about them. Some mothers, of course, didn't know about the sexual abuse. If the perpetrator was someone outside the family, your mother may not have been as likely to know about the abuse. But if it was someone within the family, particularly your father, stepfather, or your mother's boyfriend, the likelihood is great that she *did* know, consciously or unconsciously. Of course, mothers will insist that they did not know, and in a sense some will be telling the truth. They may be in so much denial that they have blocked it out of their memory. And while your mother should not be blamed for what the perpetrator did, she most likely contributed to the abuse by being what Susan Forward, in her 1978 book *Betrayal of Innocence,* called the "silent partner."

Mothers play the role of the "silent partner" in many ways. Many mothers of molested children cannot relate with their children in a meaningful way. When a child is unable to get the type of nurturing relationship with her mother that she needs, the child often seeks this emotional connection elsewhere. A father who knows that his daughter would never tell her mother, or that his wife would never believe their daughter, has only his internal inhibitions to stop him from acting on his incestuous desires.

Silent partners are often absent either physically or emotionally from the home, and this absence leaves the door wide open for child molesters. Now, a mother's physical absence in and of itself is not the cause of the abuse. Rather, it is her relinquishing of parental responsibility, her seeming nonchalance about what occurs when she is not around that distinguishes her from the typical absent mother.

Sometimes the mother plays a part in father-daughter incest (including stepfather incest) by abdicating more and more responsibilities as mother and wife to her daughter. The mother may even encourage her daughter to meet certain needs of her husband, such as keeping him company, going places with him, even rubbing his feet. It is no wonder that a daughter often gets the message from her mother that it would be helpful to satisfy her father's sexual needs to save her mother from having to do so. There are even mothers who overtly instigate the sexual encounter, giving their husband permission to use their daughter sexually with the attitude of "better her than me."

Along with being physically absent or emotionally preoccupied, these mothers tend to deny family problems. This type of woman has difficulty facing reality. She lives in a fantasy world of daydreams, sleep, books, television, drugs, or alcohol. One victim remembers her mother actually present in the same room, reading, while her father molested her! This same mother, when confronted with the truth, insisted that no such thing could have happened. "What, do you think I am blind?" she protested incredulously.

To a mother in denial, "overlooking" significant signs of abuse is commonplace. A mother of a sex-abuse victim is thus capable of "not noticing" her child's bleeding or her torn clothes following an assault, her child hiding in a corner afraid of everyone, her child having vaginal infections or red and raw genitals, her child begging not to be left alone with the perpetrator.

The mother who was molested herself as a child will often be the last one to believe that her child is also being abused. This is especially true if she never received professional help or was unable to talk to someone about her own abuse, and had thus blocked out her own memories and feelings. Some mothers don't want to help their children, since no one helped them when they were being abused themselves. As one victim's mother said, "I had to learn to fend for myself. Now I resented my daughter's demands for attention. I pushed her away because I thought, Why should she get what I never got?"

Another mother confessed, "I hate to admit this, but I actually resented the fact that my daughter had a father who seemed to care about her so much, because I never had a father around. When he started being sexual with her I thought, Well, now you don't have it so good, do you?"

Another reason why a mother sometimes plays the role of the silent partner is because she sees her daughter as competition. If she notices her husband looking at her daughter seductively, she often will blame her daughter for dressing provocatively, especially if the mother was herself molested as a child and blamed herself for it. When she sees warning signs of her husband's intentions, her attitude is more vindictive than protective: "Well, she's getting what she deserves—she shouldn't have been flaunting her body all over the place." And if the mother does acknowledge the incest, she may very likely view it as the daughter "having an affair" with her husband, rather than recognizing that her daughter is being abused and needs help.

While some mothers passively stand by, others actually promote the abuse by encouraging the child to "sleep with Daddy," "shower with Daddy," or "let Daddy touch your breasts." This kind of behavior may indicate severe emotional disturbance (often caused by childhood sexual abuse). These mothers lack the normal maternal instinct to protect, nurture, and care for their children.

Then there is the woman so afraid of losing her husband or boyfriend and ending up alone that she will do anything to keep him, to the point of allowing him to have sex with her children. The message to the male (whether verbal or unstated) is "You can do anything to me or my children; just don't leave." Often feeling sexually inadequate, she may buy into her man's complaints about "not getting enough sex." Fearful of losing him and rather than risking him going outside the marriage for sex, she may prefer him to "keep it in the family."

One of the hardest truths to face is the possibility that your mother did not really care enough about you to protect you. Many of the women in my groups have had to confront the fact that their mothers chose their father or stepfather over them, and even that their own mothers may have either molested them or actively participated in the sexual abuse. The pain of realizing any of these things is tremendous. For some, giving up the fantasy that their mother loved them is as devastating as the sexual abuse itself.

Facing the truth about your mother may leave you feeling abandoned and lost, like a "motherless child." It is not uncommon for people to feel deeply depressed and even suicidal at this time. This will be a crucial period for you—a time to nurture yourself, a time to learn to become your own supportive, loving parent. Make certain that you stay connected with your inner child by having dialogues with her and holding your stuffed animal. This may also be a time to seek outside help. And if you are feeling suicidal, *seek professional help immediately*. If you feel alone and abandoned, try reaching out to friends or a support group. If you feel depressed, know this: Depression is generally caused by two things, feelings of loss and feelings of anger. When someone is suffering from a sense of loss as you are now, it is natural and *normal* to feel a deep sadness or depression. Allow yourself to cry, to mourn the loss of your mother, or at least the loss of your fantasy mother. Hold your stuffed animal and let it comfort you. Spend time curled up in the fetal position, put pillows and stuffed animals around you as a "protective wall." Depression is also caused by suppressed and repressed anger. In the next chapter we will discuss anger and constructive ways of releasing it. Once you have released your anger, your depression will also lift.

FACING THE TRUTH ABOUT THE SEXUAL ABUSE OF CHILDREN

There are few absolute truths in life, you will find, but this is one: *Childhood sexual abuse is not just a violation of the body, but of the mind and spirit as well. It is a violation of the whole person.* And from this, the other truths follow:

- Incest and child molestation are never nonabusive; coercion is always involved in sex between an adult and child. It is never a mutual decision or agreement.
- A child never "wants" to have sex with an adult. She or he may want affection, attention, closeness, approval, or to please the adult—but never sex.
- Normal sex play and exploration occur only between those of the same age, sexual experience, and power.
- Sexual abuse is an act of violence or selfishness; it is never an act of love.
- There is no such thing as "mild" childhood sexual abuse. Childhood sexual abuse is always traumatic.

Breaking the Cycle

Sexual abuse does not occur in a vacuum, as an isolated incident. It usually occurs because of prior victimization, and it repeats itself over and over. Each person who is sexually victimized has a high chance of becoming a victimizer, and each victim touches the lives of hundreds of people. Even if a victim can refrain from abusing other children, he or she often attracts people who are child molesters. Sexually abused children can grow up to be not only sex abusers but silent partners to childhood sexual abuse as well. *Facing and telling the truth, no matter how difficult and painful, is the only way out of the cycle of abuse.* You are not at the beginning of the cycle, but with courage and determination, you can work toward ending it. Only through silence can the abuse continue.

Breaking the cycle of abuse, silence, and denial is difficult. Your family will not want their "disease" exposed. When you break into this system, you need to realize that because you haven't fully recovered from the "disease" yourself, you are particularly susceptible when you are exposed to it. Denial is contagious. When you are around people who are in denial you may start to deny again; you may start to doubt your own perceptions again.

Keep telling yourself the truth. Hold it in your heart! Truth is the only protection from denial, the only defense against deception. Like a cleansing water, the truth washes away the distortions and denial. In its place it leaves a deep sense of "knowing," a clarity and strength. The truth does indeed set us free.

Now that you know the truth, the truth is yours to use for recovery. You have a better idea of what physical and mental pain you endured and what long-term effects you are suffering from. There is healing in discovering the truth, facing it, and finally in accepting it. Your realization of the facts of the abuse clears the way for dealing with your anger and resolving your relationships with your family. You have lived with lies, secrecy, and deception for a long time, and it has been painful. Learning to live with the truth will help free you of that pain and lead you toward a richer, fuller life of recovery.

STEP 2

Releasing Your Anger

DURING YOUR RECOVERY process, many feelings will begin to surface. The emotion that will have the strongest impact on you and become your strongest ally in recovery will be anger. Yet for many of us anger can be the most threatening and frightening of all our emotions. For this reason, victims have a difficult time accepting and expressing their anger. But if they can conquer their fear, they can rise above the status of victim to survivor. Fear of anger keeps victims imprisoned by their past, afraid to stand up to those who have hurt them and afraid to go forward—to be successful, to be able to trust, and to express their sexuality.

Anger is energy, a motivating force that can empower those who feel helpless. Anger is your way out. By releasing your anger in a constructive way, you will increase your ability to *truthfully* communicate what you feel. Speaking the truth (sometimes the "angry" truth) will prevent the build-up of resentment and help release the physical and emotional tension that has sapped you of your energy—energy that could otherwise be used to feel and express love and compassion.

The more you face the truth, the angrier you will probably become. And you will be completely right in your anger with all of the following people:

the abuser
your parents
your childhood family
anyone who exposed you to the abuser
anyone who excused or protected the abuser
anyone who should have been concerned and didn't act
anyone who didn't believe you when you tried to tell
anyone who told you to forget it
anyone who blamed you
anyone who told you that you did it for your pleasure

You have a right to be angry about being sexually abused. You have a right to be angry with the perpetrator, regardless of who it was, how long ago the sexual abuse occurred, or how much he or she has changed.

You also have a right to be angry with your parents for the way they set you up for the abuse, the way they ignored or handled the situation, and for the way they mistreated and disbelieved you. You have a right to be angry with your parents no matter how difficult their childhood was. Even if they claim they "tried" to be good parents, you *still* have a right to be angry with them.

There are others you may also feel angry toward: teachers who ignored you, ministers who branded you a sinner, therapists who denied your pain or reabused you—anyone who perpetuated the cycle of lies, deceit, or denial.

THE TRUTH ABOUT ANGER

It is difficult to get past our prior conditioning about feeling angry. Our society does not give permission to express anger, even *constructively.* We are told it is a weakness to be angry, that anger feeds anger, and that it doesn't do any good to get angry.

The truth is that getting angry can actually be a strength. It takes courage to admit that you are angry rather than hiding it. It takes courage to face the person you are angry with directly and risk the consequence of rejection or retaliation rather than get back at someone indirectly, vengefully, or manipulatively. It takes no courage to push the anger down and pretend you are unaffected or don't care. That is the "safe" but unhealthy way out.

If you release your anger in an honest, direct, constructive way, your anger will dissipate. Anger stored can become a tremendously heavy burden. Releasing your anger will not change what has happened or change the other person, but it will change *you.*

Anger and blame are different. Anger is a *normal* emotional response when someone hurts or wrongs you. You are angry with the people listed above because you were abused, deprived, and disbelieved. That doesn't mean you blame them; it means you hold them accountable for their behavior. The difference between anger and blame is that blaming keeps us caught up in the problem, while releasing our anger constructively allows us to work through the problem.

Anger is neither good nor bad. What you do or don't do with the anger determines whether it is positive or negative. Later in this chapter you will read about positive ways to release your anger. These techniques will allow you to vent your anger without losing control or damaging others.

Keep in mind that there are three things you *shouldn't* do with anger:

suppress it by ignoring it;
repress it by denying or "forgetting" it;
displace it by directing it toward someone or something that is not the real cause.

Suppression. No matter how deeply we try to bury our anger, it always manages to remain just under the surface. Suppression results when we *consciously* try to forget or inhibit our anger, but it is not very effective. Because in actuality, we haven't truly "forgotten" it; we are merely ignoring it. Long-term suppressed anger can damage relationships because it inhibits us from being joyous, loving, and sexual.

Repression. Whereas suppressed anger is anger we consciously choose to ignore, repressed anger is anger we have *unconsciously* buried. Repression is a defense mechanism in which we may remove from consciousness those ideas, impulses, and feelings that are unacceptable to us. Even when we unconsciously repress our feelings, our bodies still remember them in *body memories* or body armoring. The body remembers the pain, betrayal, and invasion with stiffness, constrictions, and tension.

Repressed anger can be dangerous. It can build up inside until it finally reaches a "boiling point." We can "keep the lid on" for just so long before the pressure has to be released, all too often causing us to be abusive and violent to ourselves and others.

On the other extreme, repressed anger can cause us to become numb to our feelings altogether, so that we are no longer in contact with how we feel. We lose our enthusiasm and aliveness, and we feel tired much of the time.

Displacement. When we displace our anger we direct it to where it doesn't belong. Instead of focusing our anger where it is appropriate, we blame innocent people and get irrationally angry at circumstances or even at inanimate objects, often for no good reason. Since displaced anger does not offer a release to the appropriate target, the anger itself seldom dissipates. This results in a cycle of constantly blaming others, which makes relationships difficult.

WHY SHOULD I RELEASE MY ANGER?

Many people choose one of the above-mentioned methods of dealing with anger because they feel that they must work on "forgetting the past." But as we are learning, we cannot completely forget our past, nor can we ever successfully ignore, deny, disguise, wish away, or "forget" our anger and the sexual abuse that caused it.

Where does unexpressed anger go? It turns inward on yourself, making you feel guilty, inadequate, and worthless. Because you couldn't accept the fact that your parents or the perpetrator could do such things to you, because you couldn't accept the fact that *they* were "bad," you concluded that *you* must be the one who was bad. The anger that you internalized made you feel dark and ugly inside.

This phenomenon is particularly true in the case of incest. To a child, the idea that parents are bad is intolerable. Because children naturally tend to blame themselves for everything, children who have been sexually abused by a parent or other loved one feel that it must have been their fault. Even those who are able to recognize the perpetrator as the one responsible are usually afraid to express their anger for fear of punishment. This anger then becomes turned against themselves, causing them to become self-critical, self-destructive, and self-loathing. As the child gets older this self-blame gets carried into adulthood. When clients ask me, "How can I stop feeling guilty about the abuse?" I tell them,

"Start expressing your anger. Get angry at the ones who are really responsible."

THE DARKNESS INSIDE OF YOU ISN'T YOURS

During one group session, several women talked about how they always felt as if they had a black mark on them, as if they were damaged goods. They discussed how they felt ashamed of themselves and their bodies. This common experience causes most survivors to spend the rest of their lives trying to make up for the "bad" things they have done by being very "good" people. They try extra hard to be fair, good, and to do the "right" thing. Leslie, for example, decided to be celibate in order to prove to God that she was now a good person. Although these women realized intellectually that the abuse had not been their fault, they didn't seem to "get it" *emotionally;* they still blamed themselves.

You may have been told many times by your therapist, by your friends, and by your loved ones that the sexual abuse was not your fault, but you may still blame yourself. Releasing your anger toward the abuser will help you more than anything else to fully understand this. As you redirect your internalized anger at the abuser, keep focusing it toward him. He is the *appropriate* target for your anger. Getting angry at the abuser will affirm your innocence. Moreover, the vital force of anger will be moving in the right direction: outward instead of inward. The more you outwardly express your anger about what the abuser did to you, the better you will feel about you. Health and recovery are now in motion.

As your first step toward releasing your anger, do the following: Sit comfortably and breathe deeply. Imagine you are looking inside of your body. Find any shame or "bad" feelings you might have there. Imagine you are reaching down inside your body and pulling out all that dark, ugly stuff. Now imagine you are throwing all that dark ugliness, at the abuser, where it belongs. Open your eyes and make a throwing motion with your arms. Say out loud as you do it: *"It's not mine—it's yours."*

In addition to alleviating guilt, shame, and self-hatred, releasing your anger will do the following:

- Improve your self-esteem. When you stop blaming yourself, your self-esteem will strengthen.
- Give you hope. You will feel as if a tremendous burden has been lifted from your shoulders. It takes a huge amount of energy to hold down all that anger.
- Release physical tension. When you start releasing your anger, your body will become more relaxed, more mobile.
- Free you to express love and joy, and to experience feelings of pleasure.
- Clarify your thinking and improve your decision-making abilities. Your thinking will become less confused when you are less distracted by your anger.
- Empower you physically and emotionally and help to make you more assertive.
- Help you become an independent person, enabling you to mentally and emotionally separate from your parents and leave destructive relationships.
- Improve your relationships. You will be less likely to take your anger out on your mate, children, friends, and coworkers.
- Affirm your innocence.
- Help you to become a survivor instead of remaining a victim.

Remember that internalizing anger not only makes you feel guilty and ashamed but also causes you to punish yourself with negative relationships and self-destructive behavior (such as food, alcohol, or drug abuse, or self-mutilation with razors, knives, or pins). The incidence of eating disorders (obesity, bulimia, anorexia) is very high among victims of sexual abuse. Starving or overeating becomes a punishment for being so dirty and ugly inside. Those who are overweight are often holding in a tremendous amount of anger. In fact, they are literally "bursting at the seams" with it. Their bodies reflect the torment of their inner feelings about themselves.

Let all that self-hatred become righteous anger toward the abuser. Stop taking it out on yourself and begin taking it out *of* yourself.

One Step toward Freedom: Jackie's Story

When Jackie first came to the survivors' workshop, she could hardly talk. Only after several sessions could she get even a few sentences out, at which time she became extremely apologetic, repeating, "I'm sorry. I don't know what's wrong with me. I'm so stupid, I can't even talk." With time, it became clear that Jackie was "sorry" for even existing. Her guilt was so overwhelming that she, like many victims, often felt suicidal.

Jackie's story, revealed in bits and pieces, disclosed one of the most horrendous histories of physical, emotional, and sexual abuse imaginable. Repeatedly raped and molested by several of her mother's boyfriends, she had then been physically beaten by one of them. And yet in telling her story, Jackie did not express the slightest intimation of anger; instead, what she expressed was a great deal of guilt. Other participants' anger only bewildered her. "But my mother told me I *wanted* to have sex with those men, that I actually *asked* them for it." Jackie's mother's accusations had been so convincing that Jackie regarded all of her symptoms—self-mutilation, terrible nightmares, fear of men, an inability to speak in front of people—as merely attempts at "getting attention." In spite of her mother's obvious neglect, Jackie was convinced that she should be grateful for the maternal care she did get, that she should just forget about the past and go on.

It took a lot of therapeutic work on Jackie's part (both in group and individual therapy) to recover from the child abuse that had emotionally crippled her. But hardest and most important for her was to admit her anger toward her mother and learn nonthreatening ways of releasing it.

Because of her own physical abuse, Jackie feared any physical display of anger. But she was able to write down her angry feelings toward her mother, and the more she did this, the more in touch with reality she became. Memories and images of her childhood started coming back, reminding her of her mother's role in the abuse.

Eventually it became clear to Jackie that she was not guilty of anything. And the more she released her anger (using many of the techniques listed at the end of this chapter)—first toward her mother and finally toward the men who abused her—the less guilty she felt.

Two years later, Jackie no longer has suicidal thoughts; she has given up her self-destructive behaviors and has no more nightmares. Occasionally she becomes dizzy and disoriented, but now she understands the cause and can remedy the situation. She can now speak in front of people (even though she is still afraid), and this has resulted in a job promotion. Although she will always suffer some negative effects from her devastating childhood, she is much more self-confident and literally able to "hold her head up high." This woman who didn't think she had the right to speak, much less speak out, stopped being a victim and became a survivor.

WHY WE RESIST RELEASING OUR ANGER

Even though you may agree that releasing anger will help you toward recovery, you may still fear actually doing it. What if the perceived consequences outweigh the benefits?

Only by examining these fears can we overcome our resistance to expressing our anger and setting ourselves free.

Fear of Retaliation

Most commonly, victims fear retaliation. Even though the person who is the source of your anger need never know anything about your fury toward him, the fear can still remain. You may still be afraid of the perpetrator or of your parents, even though they have little or no actual power over you. It is actually your inner child who is afraid; that child in you may be convinced that violence always follows anger. You may be especially afraid of releasing your anger if you were physically abused as a child or if you were threatened with physical abuse whenever you became angry.

Tell your inner child that you will protect her. You do not need to expose her to the feared person. Reassure her that others have no magical powers to "know" when you are expressing your anger toward them. Release your anger a little at a time. The more you release your anger, the less afraid you will be. Tell yourself, *He can't hurt me anymore. I'm strong now.*

Fear of Hurting the Other Person

Some clients express a reluctance to release their anger for fear of hurting the other person. This is true even when that person is dead. If this is your fear, tell yourself that your anger cannot hurt them; it can hurt only you, if you continue to hold it in. For too long you have been protecting the ones who hurt you by minimizing your trauma and deprivation. It's time to stop protecting them and start protecting yourself. They have been telling you all your life that you are somehow responsible for them and their emotional well-being. You are not. You are responsible only for yourself.

Fear of Becoming Like Those Who Abused You

Another source of resistance to expressing anger is our fear that we ourselves will become abusers, monsters, even murderers. We have this fear for two reasons. First of all, if we were raised around abusive, violent people, we probably fear becoming like them (a realistic fear if we do not release our pent-up anger constructively). Second, we may be in touch with a monstrous, murderous rage inside of ourselves toward the perpetrator or our parents. We may have been holding this rage down with a vengeance, fearing that if we allow even a little to leak out, we will explode viciously and hurt them.

If you fear continuing the cycle of abuse, then there is even more of a need for you to begin *now* to start to release your anger in constructive ways—because your rage *can* destroy you and others if you continue to hold it in. But it will not destroy anyone if it is released constructively.

Fear of Losing Control

For many people, expressing anger may mean losing control. You may be afraid that once you start to vent your anger you will "go crazy" and hurt yourself or others. Ironically, as mentioned earlier, it is the person who represses her anger who is much more likely to "lose control," to become destructive, or to have the rage erupt in inappropriate ways and at inappropriate times.

Fear of losing control and becoming a wild maniac stops some people from releasing their anger. If such fear stops you, performing the following exercises should help.

Before we begin, it is important to know a little about the technique called *visualization* that will be used in both this and subsequent exercises. Visualization is the process of imagining something or bringing a mental image of it to your mind's eye. In this and the other visualization exercises in this book, visualizing a scene can make you feel as if you are actually experiencing it. This can give you valuable information as to how you would react if a particular scene literally took place. Having in a sense already experienced the situation in your mind can put you more in control. You now have a choice to actually experience the situation in real life or to avoid it. (Note: Not everyone can visualize. If you find it difficult after a couple of tries, skip to the next exercise.)

We will start off with a pleasant and simple visualization, just to acquaint you with the experience.

Visualization Warm-Up

1. Lie down or sit in a comfortable chair, relax, and close your eyes. Begin to breathe deeply and evenly. As you breathe out, say the word *one* silently to yourself. Breathe easily and naturally.
2. Deeply relax all your muscles, beginning at your feet and progressing up to your face, by first tensing them as hard as you can, and then letting go and relaxing them.
3. Now visualize a beautiful scene in nature, such as a brook in a meadow or whatever comes to mind. Really immerse yourself in this scene. Notice all the details of the scenery, and imagine that you are actually there. Enjoy the beautiful world that you have created.

Anger Visualization

Now, repeat the first three steps of the above exercise, instead of visualizing a scene in nature, do the following:

1. Visualize what you imagine might happen if you became extremely angry and totally "lost control." What

would you do? Really "see" what might happen. How does it feel?

2. After you finish visualizing this fantasy, write it down. You may want to share this visualization with your therapist, friend, or support group. Getting your fear out in the open lessens its power to influence your behavior.

Gradual Release

1. Get into a comfortable position again. Complete the relaxation steps.
2. Visualize your anger as steam that has built up in some pipes. Imagine that the steam (anger) has filled the pipes almost to the bursting point (losing control).
3. Slowly let some of the steam out of the pipes by carefully and gradually opening a valve. Allow only a small amount of steam out at a time. Eventually all the steam will be released and no pipes will burst. Your anger is the steam building up inside you. If you release your anger a little at a time, you will not lose control.

Written Exercises

Without planning answers, complete the following sentences until you have no more responses:

Losing control means . . .
I am afraid to release my anger because . . .

In all my years working as a therapist—many of those spent helping people to ventilate anger—no client has ever "lost control" while releasing anger in my office. People have pounded, kicked, yelled, thrown pillows—one client even ripped up a pillow with his bare hands. But no one "lost control" and tore up my office, lunged at me, or tried to hurt herself.

If you start releasing your anger in controlled ways, a little at a time, you will prove to yourself that you can ventilate anger without losing control.

SNEAKING PAST YOUR RESISTANCE

Getting past the resistance to your anger can sometimes prove more difficult than actually *expressing* it. If you are still reluctant to release your anger, if you feel there is some reason to hold it in that hasn't been mentioned, the following exercise is for you:

Using pen and paper, write and complete this sentence:

I don't want to release my anger because . . .

Without planning answers, continue completing the sentence until you have no more responses. If you need help, your therapist or a trusted friend can assist you.

Sometimes clients say that they know they *should* be angry at the perpetrator or their family, but they just don't *feel* it. Since it is often easier to get angry about someone else's abuse than it is to get angry at your own, imagine how you would feel if you had a child who was sexually abused. Would you get angry? Do you feel angry when you think of how many children are abused in this country? Do you feel angry when you hear other victims' stories? Let the anger you feel about the abuse of others prime you for the anger you deserve to feel about your own abuse.

You can also "sneak by" your resistance and fear by finding ways to begin releasing your anger as part of your daily schedule. For instance, while you are cleaning the house, do any of the following:

- While shaking out the rugs, envision yourself saying to the abuser or your parents, "Get out of my life."
- Each time you reach forward with the vacuum cleaner, call out, "Get away from me."
- When taking out the garbage, stomp on the egg cartons, aluminum cans, or any other garbage that makes a loud sound and imagine you are stomping on whoever hurt you.
- If you do carpentry, pound each nail with a "Take that!"
- If you do gardening, release your anger as you hoe the soil, cut limbs, or tear out weeds.

If you cannot find a way to physically release your anger, it will stay stored up in your body until you do release it. Take a close look at your resistance to physically releasing your anger. It may remind you of your own abuse. Sometimes the sound of hitting, even when you are the one in control, can cause you to relive your own abuse. A good way of avoiding this trauma is to make certain that you focus on doing the hitting, not on receiving the hits. Victims are sometimes still afraid of the perpetrator, even though they know he is not physically present. A technique used in some groups is to picture the perpetrator securely tied up and gagged. If you imagine you are hitting him or yelling at him, you will feel safer knowing he cannot hurt you.

Whichever anger-release technique you use, be prepared for more resistance on your part. Resistance will take many different forms: worrying about what other people will think; feeling too tired right after you've started; worrying about hurting your back, blistering your hands, feeling silly, and so on. If you really get into an exercise and start ventilating your anger in an intense way, be assured that you won't feel tired, you won't feel silly, and you won't worry about getting blisters—you will be so caught up in the moment that you will not even be aware of these things. And after you have spontaneously "let go," you will feel renewed and relieved, as if a heavy burden has been lifted.

You can find lots of excuses for not releasing your anger. There will always seem to be a better time. Don't fool yourself! There is no better time than now!

Remember: Resisting releasing your anger is like resisting recovery!

PREPARING TO RELEASE YOUR ANGER

So far in this section we have investigated different anger-release techniques: visualization and fantasizing, writing, verbalizing, and physical releasing. Finding the best anger-release technique for yourself may take some experimentation. You may find several that work for you at different times, situations, and places. If, for example, you get angry while at work, you may not be able to release it physically. If your body wants to hit but you have no way to do it, *imagine you are hitting*. Then you can wait until you get home to do some actual physical playing out if you still need to. Fantasizing and imagining can be an emotional release in itself, although it does not replace physical exertion in terms of reducing physical tension. Fantasizing or imagining can also be an effective way of preparing yourself for some actual physical release. The more you can imagine yourself releasing your anger, the more able you will be to do it.

Try at least one exercise from each category, then choose the method or methods that seem to fit your needs and personality. If physical violence frightens you or repulses you, you may prefer to release your anger in a nonphysical way, such as letter writing. Keep in mind, however, that those who have experienced a physical trauma to the body such as sexual abuse will usually need to release their anger physically at some point.

Your body can give you clues as to what type of physical

release would be best for you. Ask yourself, "What does my body usually feel like doing when I am angry? Does it feel like kicking, hitting, throwing things, or screaming?" If you feel like hitting, it may be because you have been holding your anger in the parts of the body that are involved with hitting—your shoulders, neck, arms, hands, and back.

Note that if you answered, "My body feels like crying when I am angry," you are probably not attending to your feelings of anger. Crying is *not* an adequate way of releasing *anger;* crying is the way to express pain and sadness. Victims in general and women in particular often cry when they are really feeling angry. You may have been allowed to cry when you were a child but severely punished if you showed any anger.

ANGER-RELEASE TECHNIQUES

Caution: If you have been suicidal, have a history of severe emotional problems, or have been hospitalized for such difficulties, have your therapist or a friend present when you release anger through any of these physical techniques. They can give you any reassurance or assistance needed.

Physical Exercises

In all the physical releases, inhale deeply before making any sudden exertion and remember to keep breathing. Let out a sound with each exhale whenever you can; say *no* or another word that expresses your anger. You might place a picture of the person you are angry with nearby when engaged in some of the physical releases.

Hitting

1. Purchase an "encounter bat" or "bataca" (a foam bat available in most sporting-goods stores) or use a plastic bat or old tennis racquet. Place a large pillow before you on the floor or position yourself on or next to your bed. Get on your knees, lift the bat directly over your head, and come down hard in a swift thrust. You can envision the person you are angry with, but as you hit make sure your eyes are wide open and focused on a spot on the pillow or bed.
2. Punch a punching bag or punch the air as in shadow boxing.
3. Pound pillows with your fists. Lie down on your back on the floor or on your bed. Place pillows at your sides, directly under your hands.
4. Hit a piece of furniture with a rolled-up towel, newspaper, or magazine.
5. Play a sport that requires a hitting action, such as tennis, racquetball, or volleyball. Focus on releasing anger while you are hitting.
6. Sock or punch clay, dough, or any other pliable material.

Kicking and Stomping

1. Stomp on old egg cartons or aluminum cans.
2. Kick a large pillow or ball.
3. Take a walk; each time you take a step imagine you are stomping on the person you are angry with.
4. Practice karate kicks.
5. On a bed or mat, do scissor kicks.

Pushing

1. Place two large pillows against a wall. Lie on your back. Using your feet and legs, kick and push the pillows as hard as you can against the wall. (This is especially effective for women who have been raped or violently assaulted.)
2. Facing a wall or door, stand with your arms straight out in front of you, an arm's length from the wall or door. With feet planted firmly on the ground, start pushing as hard as you can against the wall. Say out loud, "Get away from me," or "Leave me alone."

Throwing

1. Throw unwanted dishes, raw eggs, or water balloons against your garage wall, back fence, or garbage can.
2. Throw pillows against the wall. Make sure to let out a sound like "No!" or "Get away!" or "Take that!" as you do so.
3. Throw balls or darts.
4. Throw rocks into a river or into the ocean.

Tearing

1. Tear an old phone book or newspapers into pieces.
2. Tear up old pillows, sheets, or rags.

Screaming and Yelling

1. Put your face into a pillow and scream as hard as you can.
2. Yell and scream in the shower.
3. Turn the TV or radio up loud and scream.

4. Scream and yell on amusement park "thrill" rides.
5. Scream long and loud in a quiet, private place.
6. Roll up your car windows, turn your radio up loud, and scream as long and hard as you can.

Writing Exercises

In the following exercises, write whatever comes to your mind. Don't censor yourself. Remember that no one will ever need to see what you have written.

Expressing Anger

1. Write a letter to the person you are angry with, expressing exactly how you feel. This letter is intended for releasing anger, not for mailing. Don't ask *questions* like "How could you . . .?" or "Why did you . . .?" Questions help maintain your role as victim. Instead, make *statements* using "I," such as "I'm angry with you for what you did . . ." or "I don't like what you did . . ." Be assertive. When you are done, you may either tear up the letter or keep it. (When you move to the next step of confronting, you may ultimately decide to mail it.)
2. Complete each of the following sentences:

   I am angry at the perpetrator because . . .
   I am angry at my mother/father because . . .
   I am angry at my sibling(s) because . . .
   I am angry at______because . . .

Fantasizing and Imagining Exercises

For some people, it may be easier to *imagine* releasing their anger rather than doing it through physical or written exercises.

Verbalizing Anger

1. Have an imaginary conversation with the person you are angry with. Tell that person exactly how you feel; don't hold back anything.
2. Pretend the person you are angry with is sitting in a chair across from you. It may help to put a picture of the person on the chair. Talk to the empty chair or the picture and "tell off" that person.
3. Express your feelings of anger into a tape recorder.

All of these anger-release techniques can create lasting results if you practice them regularly. Once any initial resistance is overcome, you will soon experience the positive effects of releasing anger that were listed earlier in this chapter.

COPING WITH OTHERS' RESISTANCE

Your family and friends may not understand why you have to release your anger. They may try to talk you out of your anger with statements like "It's un-Christianlike" or "It's unhealthy." They will tell you that you should forgive instead of holding a grudge, that there is nothing to be gained from getting angry.

It is *not* okay to "live and let live," to "let bygones be bygones," to "forgive and forget," to "let the past be the past," or any of the other clichés your family and friends will use to persuade you to forget about what happened and go on. Instead of accepting these messages, use your anger as a source of strength to answer them:

- The past is *not* past; it is still here, ruining my life.
- I'm not trying to change the past, I'm changing the way I'm dealing with it.

- I'm angry because I was hurt. I can't work on forgiving until I release that anger.
- I have a right to be angry. If you really want to help me, you will try to encourage me to release it.

Some people may be afraid that you will get hurt by releasing your anger. Others will try to discourage you from releasing your anger because they are more comfortable with you as a weak and passive victim. When you become angry you become powerful, and they cannot control you. And they fear your anger because they fear their own; your anger will only stir up their own unresolved feelings.

No one has the right to tell you it is not okay to be angry. It is *always* appropriate to be angry about being sexually abused. It is never too late to feel the rage. Nothing anyone can say should stand in your way of releasing your anger. So get angry. Your recovery depends on it.

STEP 3

Confronting with Facts and Feelings

THIS WAS AN important day for Nancy. She had been preparing for it for months. Today she was going to confront her father about sexually abusing her from age three to age twelve. I had been expecting a large and powerful man, since that is how Nancy had described him. Instead, I was greeted by a small, rather pathetic-looking person who stood up when I entered the waiting room but was unable to look me in the eye.

What occurred during the next twenty minutes included one of the best displays of dauntless courage I have observed. Nancy confronted her father with the truth of his abuse, including how she had been affected. When her father tried to deny it, she looked at him steadily and said, "I didn't expect you to tell the truth, but I *know* what happened to me. I have the flashbacks to prove it. You may not have thought a little toddler would remember—you may have even thought it wouldn't affect me. But it did—it has affected me *severely.*"

Her father was stunned. He tried to manipulate her by feigning innocence and even by accusing me of "putting these ideas into her head," but Nancy stood firm. Suddenly, her father's quiet demeanor metamorphosed, and he began to verbally attack her. "You don't know what you are talking about. You're crazy!" he said. "There was something wrong with you even as a child." The façade of the downtrodden father fell away as his anger surfaced. And as his face, contorted with rage, revealed a man who was very emotionally disturbed, the small, pathetic gentleman from the waiting room transformed into the large and seemingly powerful bully whom Nancy had been frightened of for so many years.

Nancy was clearly shaken, but she continued. "No, I am *not* crazy. I am the sanest one in our family. And as far as there being something wrong with me as a child—of *course* there was. I was being sexually abused by you from the time I was just a little girl!"

Her father was still trying to regain his composure after his outburst, and now these last words from Nancy seemed to leave him literally speechless. He was visibly angry, but he had already exposed his rage to me once and didn't seem to want to do it again. His daughter had stood up to him for the first time. He had lost face in front of me, his authority had been challenged, and he was being forced to hear the truth. He couldn't stand it any longer. He got up and walked out. Nancy turned to me and said, "I think that's the only time in his life when he let someone else have the last word."

Even though her father did not admit the truth, Nancy felt that the confrontation was still worthwhile. She felt proud for being able to confront him in spite of the fact that she had been so frightened. For the first time, his efforts to try to intimidate or confuse her had not worked because she was certain of the *truth.* She had stood up to him, and now she no longer feared him. Nancy's confrontation was a powerful step in her process toward recovery.

Of course, it is not necessary (or even desirable) for everyone to actually confront the perpetrator face-to-face. But you will need to find your own way of confronting your perpetrator and anyone else who abused you, betrayed you, or set you up. Your confrontation can be by telephone, in a letter, or just in your imagination. The *method* of confrontation is not nearly as important as is your finding a way to do it.

A confrontation is a way of formally challenging someone with the truth about what happened as well as with your feelings about it. It is *not* necessarily an attack; it is not meant to alienate others. It is also not an argument. Its purpose is not to change anyone or to necessarily force agreement with you, or belief in you. A confrontation is merely a statement of *facts* and *feelings*.

Confronting is different from releasing your anger. Part of your confrontation will undoubtedly include relating your anger, but this is not the primary purpose. Instead, your purpose is to stand up to those who have hurt you, to tell them how they hurt you and how you feel about them. You can confront without being angry, just as you can release your anger without necessarily confronting. In fact, it is important that you ventilate your anger *before* you confront, so that you can communicate your feelings in a strong, clear, self-assured manner. You will also be less likely to explode or lose control. It is strongly recommended that you write an "anger letter," as described in the previous chapter, before you do any confronting. From this letter you can glean the material for your confrontation. Confronting is a way to *resolve* or bring *closure* to the relationships that plague you most (with the perpetrator, with your parents, with your siblings). Once these feelings are expressed, you are guaranteed to feel better about yourself and may feel better about the relationship.

Bringing closure is important for these reasons. First, unresolved relationships will continue to bother you until you get things out in the open and deal with them, giving room for healing to occur. The internal conflict over how and if you should confront can cause you to have continual imaginary conversations with the perpetrator or your family, obsessing about how they would react, what they might say. This kind of obsessing resolves nothing.

Second, if you don't confront those who have hurt you, you will always have an emotional connection to them even if you don't want it. Confronting will help you to *disconnect* from them, once and for all.

On the other hand, confronting is a way of reaching out in love to those you wish to continue relating to. No matter how angry you are with your parents, you still love them. No matter how much they have hurt you, deep down inside you still want to be close to them. Confronting provides an opportunity to "set the record straight," to communicate what you need from them now. Confronting those who have hurt you not only gives them another chance but presents you with another chance to resolve the most important relationships you will probably ever have.

Finally, if you don't have a confrontation with those who have hurt you, you will tend to have inappropriate confrontations with others instead. You may unconsciously attribute characteristics to others that are not really theirs, or you will become attracted to people similar to those who hurt you.

BENEFITS OF CONFRONTING

Confronting those who have hurt you enables you to take back your power, proving to yourself that you are no longer going to allow anyone to frighten or control you. Confronting those who have caused you damage and pain can guarantee that you will not continue to be victimized again.

Marcy reported that every time she saw her brother he still tried to molest her as he had when she was a child, even though they were both grown and married. Only when she finally confronted him did she feel strong enough around him to hold her own. The confrontation occurred at her niece's wedding reception. As usual, Marcy's brother had begun to look at her in a sexual way. She knew that it wouldn't be long before he would start following her around and putting his hands all over her. But this time she was determined to stop him. As soon as he touched her she turned, looked him straight in the eye, and said, "I don't want you to touch me *anymore.* You sexually abused me when I was a child, and I have been suffering from it ever since. I am not going to be your victim any longer."

He told her he always thought she liked it, and that he still felt attracted to her after all these years and thought she felt the same. Marcy told him that she had *always* hated it but that she was afraid of him. She also told him that she was in therapy and that he needed help as well. From that day on, she was not afraid to be around her brother. He generally kept a respectable distance from her and stopped looking at her seductively. He didn't enter therapy, however, and so she limited their relationship to family functions only.

When you confront, you break the cycle of victimization. If, for example, one of your parents stood silently by while the other abused you, that parent's passivity deprived you of adequate parenting every bit as much as the abusive parent's actions did. With a silent partner as a role model, many victims of childhood sexual abuse thus grow up to be silent partners themselves. Confronting, however, can offer an alternative to passivity. You do not need to be impotent, passive, and ineffectual like the silent partner and *allow* things to happen. Instead, you can experience personal power, use self-control, and communicate effectively—if you confront.

Incest usually occurs in dysfunctional families. Therefore, the entire family needs to be involved in the recovery process. Confronting your family is one step toward that recovery, a way of breaking through the denial, of opening up the lines of communication, and of restructuring the family system.

Preparing for Your Confrontation

Practice your confrontation by writing it down, speaking into a tape recorder, or just talking out loud. Use the following suggested format as a guide. Once you've completed your own version, you may pick and choose those points you wish to include in your actual confrontation.

1. List what your abuser or your family did to make you feel angry, hurt, damaged, guilty, ashamed, and afraid. State every abuse, injustice, injury, damage, and painful memory you have.

   Examples

   You robbed me of my innocence.
   You betrayed my trust.
   You didn't protect me.

2. List how you felt as a result of their behavior.

   Examples

   Angry Used
   Afraid Isolated
   Guilty Worthless

3. List what effect your abuser's or your family's actions (or inaction) had on you, and how your life has been affected. Include both childhood effects and reverberations you experience as an adult.

   Examples

   As a child:
   It affected my ability to trust.
   It caused me to live in fear.
   It made me feel stupid in school.

   As an adult:
   It has caused me to be self-destructive.
   It has destroyed my feelings of self-worth and eroded my self-esteem.
   It has affected my sexuality and my health.

4. Tell them how you feel about them *now* and why.

Examples

I feel angry with you for damaging my life.
I feel afraid you will let me down again.
I am afraid you will molest my children.

5. List everything you would have wanted from your abuser or your family at the time.

Examples

I wanted you to protect me.
I wanted to be able to trust you.
I wanted you to stop.

6. List everything you want from them *now*.

Examples

I want you to listen to me and believe me.
I want you to get help.
I want you to stay away from my children.

CONFRONTING YOUR PARENTS

You will need to decide whether to confront your parents together or separately. If your parents act as if they are "joined at the hip," with neither one having an independent thought from the other, you might as well deal with them as such. In addition, having both of your parents present to hear what you have to say will guarantee that they both receive an accurate message, avoiding any "misunderstandings" or alternate versions of the story. Keep in mind, however, that by confronting them together you risk them overwhelming you. With each other for support it is possible that they could take on a stronger, more stubborn stance. It might therefore be to your advantage to talk to them separately, when each is more vulnerable and perhaps more receptive. Be aware, though, that even if you confront the silent partner alone, she may be so closely attached to the perpetrator that she will protect him no matter what he has done.

Confronting Your Mother

The first person most people think about breaking the silence to is their mother. Why is it important to confront your mother with the truth? Because no matter what she has done to you, she is still probably the most powerful connection to your past. And because the sexual abuse has created a wedge between you and your mother that has never mended, you probably blame her for the abuse. An important part of your recovery is facing your anger and allowing it to surface so you can work it through.

Confronting your mother will involve two steps: (1) confronting her with the truth; and (2) confronting her with your feelings toward her concerning the abuse. This may be done at two separate times or at once.

Confronting her with the truth. You'll need to tell your mother that you were sexually abused in order to ascertain whether she already knows, whom she blames for it, and how she feels about it. Her reactions when you tell her will reveal a lot. She may get defensive or deny it happened, blame you for not telling her sooner, or blame you for the abuse itself.

Telling your mother that your father, stepfather, or her boyfriend molested you will be especially difficult. You may be worried about destroying the feelings your mother has for the perpetrator. Many mothers already know the truth or suspect as much but have been hiding from it, so you may not actually shock her as much as you might think. Many victims fear that telling their mother about their father molesting them will break up the parents' marriage. All too often, however, nothing will cause a victim's mother to leave her husband—not even proof that he molested their child. That is, unless she already wanted out of the marriage; then she may use this information as an excuse to leave what she may have only tolerated for years.

If you are protecting your mother from knowing that her own father or brother molested you, remember that they may have also molested her when *she* was a child. If she were to face the fact that you were abused, she might then be forced to remember her own abuse; this may explain her possible denial. On the other hand, your disclosure may force her out of a lifetime denial that is not only unhealthy but potentially dangerous to any other family children who may be candidates for further victimization.

Ultimately, there are many more reasons for telling your mother than for not telling her. Disclosing will help you to discover the truth. It will unburden you of the guilt you have been carrying around to name the perpetrator and put the blame where it belongs. (It may even relieve your mother of her burden of guilt, since most mothers know on some level, especially in cases of incest.) It may save other children from being victimized by the same man, and it *may* help you and your mother to achieve a closeness never possible before. In any case, it will help you to face who your mother really is. If she is any kind of mother at all, she will want to know about your pain.

Confronting her with your feelings. Most sexual-abuse victims focus their anger on their mother first, before they can even acknowledge their anger at the perpetrator (assuming the mother was not the abuser). This is partly because of their fear of the perpetrator, but also because they feel so betrayed by their mother. Mothers are expected to protect us. That is why when you first realize the truth about your mother—whether she didn't protect you, or didn't care enough to stop the abuse or even encouraged it—the betrayal you feel can be as devastating as the sexual abuse itself. It has been my experience that the conflict of feeling both love and hate toward one's mother is probably one of the most difficult problems victims have to face during recovery. Complete healing from the terrible wounds of sexual abuse usually does not come until this conflict has been resolved one way or another, through either reconciliation or complete separation. In most cases of incest by the father, an especially painful estrangement exists between a mother and her victimized daughter.

If your mother feels you are blaming her for the sexual abuse itself, she will naturally become defensive. It will be difficult for her to accept responsibility for something she has not actually done. Try to distinguish the anger you feel toward your mother from the anger you feel toward the perpetrator. She doesn't deserve *all* the blame. Unless she was the abuser, she is responsible only for her part in the abuse, not the actual abuse itself.

If the abuse occurred while she was in the same house with you, if it was done in front of her, or if you showed obvious signs and symptoms of abuse that she ignored, then you definitely have a right to hold her accountable for her actions. Did your mother *participate* in the abuse, or did she walk in on it and then ignore it? Do you feel she set you up for the abuse by withholding love and affection, and in so doing made you a prime candidate for abuse? Then you have an obligation to your recovery to confront her.

While it makes sense to begin with the expression of your anger toward your mother, don't neglect your feelings of anger toward the abuser. The abuser is often so successful at creating that wedge between mother and child that many victims remain angrier with their mothers than they do with the perpetrator himself.

CONFRONTING YOUR SIBLINGS

In addition to confronting your parents and the perpetrator, you may need to confront other members of your family: your siblings, your grandparents, your aunts, uncles, or cousins. Just as your mother may deny your abuse or become defensive for herself or the perpetrator, the same may be true for other members of your family.

The most startling reactions can come from your siblings. Often, even a sibling whom you know was also molested by the same person will deny his or her own abuse and get angry with you for accusing the perpetrator. The fact that you may have been witness to that abuse, or that your sibling may have previously confided the abuse to you will bear no weight. *The most avid supporters of the abuser are often the ones who were also victimized,* because they are *in denial* about their own abuse.

It is a fact that fathers who sexually abuse one girl (and sometimes boy) in the family often abuse others as well. Some fathers start with the oldest and work their way down, abusing each child when that child reaches a certain age. The chances are high that your sister or brother may also have been sexually victimized by your father or that some attempt may have been made to do so. She may have "forgotten" it as a way of coping, blocking her own abuse completely either because it was so traumatic or because she didn't want to have to face the truth about her father.

You are a threat. You are bringing it all back up again. *You are the enemy!* Don't be surprised if she expresses hatred, threatens you, or refuses to see you. She may very well say something like, "You're crazy," "You're just trying to start trouble," "Daddy would *never* do such a thing," "How could you hurt mother like this?"

On the other hand, your siblings may have an entirely different perception of what life was like when you were children. Even though they experienced the same things you did—deprivation; neglect; emotional, verbal, or physical abuse—they may have played a different role in the family or developed a different way of coping, and therefore they may perceive the situation very differently from you. For example, an abusive parent may have become progressively worse, and so older children may not have suffered as much abuse as younger ones. Or the reverse could hold: The parent may have "mellowed with age" or stopped drinking and treated the younger children better. Sometimes one or both parents will favor one child over the others, or will dislike and single out one child. Any of these variables can contribute to each sibling having a different perception of what their childhood was like.

If you already know that your sibling adores your father, be aware that he or she will have an emotional investment in not believing you when you confront them with the truth. If the perpetrator was another sibling, a grandparent, uncle, or any other relative or close family friend, your sister or brother may defend him in the same way.

If your father (or any other perpetrator) did *not* sexually abuse your sibling, and if that sibling acknowledges that the abuse to you in fact occurred, you still may not get any support. This sibling may feel jealous of the "attention" you got from the perpetrator. Not understanding what was actually going on, she or he may have seen you as being the perpetrator's "favorite" and resented you as a result. On the other hand, some siblings may feel tremendous guilt for failing to protect you or for neglecting to tell someone about what was happening; they may even wish that *they* had been the ones abused and hurt instead of you. Others may withhold support out of fear. Siblings who were not abused often lived in fear that they would be next. This is especially true if they were in the same room while the abuse was occurring. Even now, as adults, they may still be so afraid of the perpetrator that they refuse to support you for fear of making the perpetrator angry with them.

Nonetheless, it is for *your* recovery process that you are doing the confronting. Don't be held back by your siblings' reactions.

CONFRONTING THE PERPETRATOR

The nature of the dynamics in confronting the actual abuser is more complicated for many victims than confronting their mother is. Clients have often expressed to me different reasons for wanting to confront their abuser directly. The most common is to punish him or to get revenge. They want to threaten him with exposure; they want to "make him squirm." They want him to know how it feels to be scared, uncertain, and controlled.

These are *not* good reasons to confront. To begin with, as far as making the perpetrator feel afraid, it is important to realize that many abusers do not feel much of *anything;* they are very often detached from their emotions. Next, if you really think you can "teach him a lesson," you are probably fooling yourself: perpetrators rarely believe they did anything wrong. Many are what we call sociopathic or antisocial, meaning that they have little sense of right and wrong. They justify their actions, blame others, and deny any wrongdoing a great majority of the time. They have much more of a need to make themselves look good than they do to help you by admitting the truth or by admitting it was wrong.

You must face this. There probably is no way for you to "get to him" or to punish him for what he did to you. Your fantasy of making him suffer like you did will probably have to remain just that—a fantasy. He will probably never be punished adequately for what he did to you. Seldom is there justice in this situation.

Some people choose to confront the perpetrator directly because they see it as a challenge: "I'm not going to allow him to continue to intimidate me any longer." Sometimes they need to show the perpetrator they are no longer afraid of him in order to stop him from continuing to victimize them. Other people need to prove to *themselves* that they are not afraid, that they are strong enough to do it; it may come down to being an ultimate personal test of strength and courage. There may be a compelling belief that a confrontation is necessary once and for all in order to recover.

Some of my clients have wanted to confront the perpetrator in order to continue a relationship with him. This is often the case when the perpetrator is the father. Many clients have been shocked to learn that they still care about the perpetrator, in spite of what he did to them. It doesn't mean you are crazy or perverted if you feel this way. It is natural to love and hate the perpetrator at the same time. You can love him for the times he was there for you, for his affection when you needed it so desperately. You can hate him for turning affection into sexuality and tricking you into doing things that hurt you emotionally and physically.

Very often, even though it may not be discussed openly, victims want to confront the perpetrator because they hope he will be sorry. This does happen *occasionally.* Sometimes a father, in his attempt to maintain or reestablish a relationship with his child, will finally admit that he abused her, that he was wrong for doing it, that it was not her fault, and that he is sorry. This is, of course, what every victim wants and needs. But don't fool yourself: It happens in only the rarest of instances. Protect yourself, and do not expect even the slightest acknowledgment of the fact that it happened. Someone as used to lying as he is is unlikely to tell you the truth now. It is far more likely that he will try to confuse you, disarm you, or make you feel like you are crazy. He will probably twist your words and manipulate the situation so much that you may even begin to doubt *yourself.* And in the unlikely event that he does acknowledge the truth to you, it is almost guaranteed that he will not admit it to anyone else.

In spite of all this, you may still choose to confront the perpetrator. If it seems important to you for whatever reasons, follow your feelings, but be aware of the possible consequences. And be prepared for the worst.

Before you confront the perpetrator, you need to consider several things. First of all, while the adult part of you may be strong and courageous, the child part of you may still be terrified of him. This means that just hearing his voice or seeing him look at you in a certain way may force you back into a childlike state again. He may be able to disarm and overpower you within minutes with just a few well-chosen words. However, the adult part of you may be able to offer protection from him. If you are able to maintain your composure long enough to actually confront him, you may find that you are confused by his reaction. Again, the child part of you may still believe everything he says, even though your logical adult self knows better. You may start doubting the truth, minimizing how much he hurt you, or start blaming yourself.

Remember, he was very convincing when you were a child. He talked you into believing that he loved you and that sex was a way of showing love. He's convinced others that you were lying, that you instigated it, that it wasn't as bad as you've said. He very likely has talked other children into sex as well. You may become so confused and disoriented that you end up not knowing what the truth is all over again.

So be prepared. Practice for the encounter. Imagine he is sitting in an empty chair across from you, and tell him how you feel. Then switch chairs and imagine you are him. Respond in the way you honestly think he would. Practice responding to his insults, denials, rationalizations, and threats. You can also use your group or your therapist or your friend to rehearse telling him off. Have another person role-play him and respond in an attacking or disarming way. Confronting the perpetrator can have strong positive rewards *if you are prepared.* Otherwise it may be disappointing and feel like a setback.

DIRECT CONFRONTATIONS

These confrontations include face-to-face encounters, telephone conversations, or letters that you mail. Unlike ventilating anger, confrontations are most effective when done face-to-face. Unfortunately, this is not always possible. It may be too dangerous if there is a risk of being reabused. Some victims of abuse have extraordinarily disturbed parents and families. Often the perpetrator is violent and insane and can still do you harm. It may be, too, that the person being confronted is medically or psychologically incapable of withstanding a confrontation. Or perhaps he or she is geographically distant or even deceased.

If a face-to-face confrontation is not possible or is too threatening, there are other ways to confront directly: You can write and then mail a letter, you can record your thoughts and send or give the tape to the person, or you can do your confronting on the telephone. Each method has its advantages and disadvantages.

If it will not endanger you, and if it is at all possible, direct confrontation will be particularly valuable if the following conditions exist:

- If the perpetrator or your family continues to abuse you verbally, emotionally, physically, or sexually.
- If you can't be around them without feeling "crazy," confused about the abuse, or doubtful of your perceptions. Confronting may help you to think and feel more clearly and should enable you to trust your own perceptions.
- If you don't feel like a separate enough person, or if you are so enmeshed with them that their opinions become yours, and you find you don't "know your own mind" when you are around them.
- If you are still afraid of them.
- If you need to protect your children or other children from them.

Before you confront directly, you will need to prepare yourself in a number of ways:

1. Take the edge off your anger through anger-releasing techniques.
2. Have clear in your mind the declarations you made at the beginning of this chapter under the exercise "Preparing for Your Confrontation." This will help you to do the following things:
   - Review the truth.
   - Clarify what your intentions are and what you want, if anything.
   - Choose what you will say about the person's actions and your feelings about the past and present.
   - Anticipate what your response will be—as a statement of fact, not as a threat—if you don't get what you want.
3. Be ready to end the confrontation whenever you decide its effectiveness is over.
4. Practice your confrontation by writing it, taping it, or just going over it aloud.
5. Be aware of the possible consequences.

Once you have laid the general groundwork, you will need some more specific preparation for a face-to-face confrontation:

1. Decide when and where you would like to have the confrontation. Where would you feel most comfortable, secure, and confident? Some people prefer their own turf; others prefer one that is neutral. Some would rather meet in a public place such as a park so that they can get away if need be. You may want the confrontation to take place in your therapist's office.

2. Be sure to have some type of support system at hand; you'll need someone to talk with after the confrontation.
3. Decide whether you would like to have a third party present. If you are apprehensive about violence or loss of control, you may need this—even if it is your *own* rage or loss of control that you fear.
4. Set some ground rules for the confrontation and determine how you will actually express them to whomever you're confronting. Here are some examples:
   - I want you to hear me out before you respond.
   - I don't want you to interrupt me or stop me.
   - I don't want you to defend, justify, or rationalize.

   Obtain a commitment from the person you are going to confront *before* you proceed: "Are you willing to give me your word to listen to me and to remain quiet until I am finished?"

Remember, you have the advantage. You have decided when, where, and under what circumstances the confrontation takes place. You are prepared; he or she is not. If you feel threatened or lose control, you can end the exchange immediately.

Face-to-Face Confrontations

Advantages. One advantage is that you see the person's reactions to what you are saying. This can help you to discover how the person really feels (about what you are saying, about what occurred, about you). It is also harder for the other person to ignore what you are saying. If the other person is receptive, there is an opportunity to talk it out at length. You will also gain a tremendous amount of self-respect. You will probably never feel like a victim again.

Disadvantages. First, there is the risk of being reabused. *You are not a coward if you can't confront face-to-face.* In addition, you may feel trapped once you have had your say because you may feel unable to leave. The person you confront may start berating you and cause you to suddenly feel confused or frightened. Keep in mind you may *not* want to know what the other person's response is. You may just want to "say your piece" without hearing a reaction. Also, the other person's response may confuse you or distract you, and you may end up saying things you really don't mean. Or, you may find that the other person is too busy thinking up a defense to actually hear what you have to say.

Telephone Confrontations

The telephone is also an effective tool if you are not prepared for a face-to-face confrontation.

Advantages. You have the benefit of being able to verbally express yourself without having to see the other person. Talking on the phone may make you feel safer and freer. If the other person becomes abusive, you can just hang up. If he or she starts to play on your sympathies, you can more effectively block this out and continue. You may also catch the person "off guard" and thus less prepared for battle.

Disadvantages. Being unable to see the person's face, you may not know what impact your words are having. Often someone's facial expression may not match his words; you will miss these important clues to what is really being said. You may get hung up on, and this could leave you feeling even more angry. Remember that you are not assured of privacy; your confrontee might have someone else nearby who could influence his response. Finally, you may catch the person at an "off" time, setting yourself up for rejection or further hurt if the person is preoccupied, hurried, or in other ways distracted.

Letters of Confrontation

It is always good to write down your feelings. Compose a practice confrontation letter. Follow the basic confrontation format if you wish, or just write from your heart. It may take you several sittings.

If you choose to send it, it may be a good idea to have someone else read it first. Your therapist and members of your group will be able to tell you how the letter sounds and make any suggestions. Keep in mind, though, that you are the ultimate judge of what you want to say and whether what you have written communicates that effectively.

Advantages. Some people have a difficult time expressing their feelings in person, especially when they feel "on the spot." Writing your feelings down may enable you to communicate them more effectively. You can rewrite until you get it right. Sometimes other people have an easier time taking in what we have to say if they read it rather than hear it. Also, something written is less likely to be misunderstood; it's right there in black and white.

Disadvantages. If you don't hear back from the person you mailed the letter to, you may feel "unfinished." You may be left waiting for a letter that never comes.

The following is a letter written by a client to her incestuous father:

> Dear Dad,
>
> I am in therapy with a woman who specializes in working with adults who were sexually abused as chil-

dren. I have had to seek professional help because of the emotional damage you caused me by sexually molesting me when I was eight years old. Yes, Dad, I do remember it all. I wasn't too young to remember like you may have thought, and I wasn't asleep, though I pretended to be because I was so afraid and ashamed.

Although I am getting better with the help of therapy, I need you to come into therapy with me so we can work on trying to mend our relationship. I don't know if I can ever forgive you, but I am willing to try.

I need to resolve this, Dad, not just for our relationship, but for my marriage. You see, Dad, because of what you did, I am unable to have sex with my husband.

If you love me and want to work this out, please call this number and make an appointment with my therapist.

Love, Diane

Much to her surprise, Diane's father did agree to come into therapy with her. He admitted what he had done and listened to Diane express her feelings about it. He also agreed to start individual therapy himself to discover why he had molested his daughter and to ensure that he never molested another child. Diane and her father are now much closer to each other, and there is definite hope for recovery and reconciliation.

Next is another confrontation letter, which had different but also beneficial results:

Dear Dad,

I am angry with you for sexually molesting me when I was a child. I know you remember it, so don't bother to deny it. I want you to know how it affected me. I felt betrayed by you. I always loved you so much, I always trusted you so much. You told me you loved me too, and I believed you. Now I don't believe anyone anymore when they say they care about me. I always think they want something from me like you did. You didn't care about my feelings, what it would do to me. Well, I'll tell you what it did to me—it ruined my childhood, prevented me from enjoying sex with my husband, and it made me angry and mean and cold to other people. I have physically abused my own children because I was so angry with you.

There is no excuse for what you did. I want you to admit what you have done and acknowledge to me that you know it was wrong. I want you to apologize to me for what you did and ask me to forgive you—but only if you really mean it. I also want you to go into therapy or to a support group like Parents United so you won't abuse other children. If you don't seek help, I can't and won't see you again. I still love you, but I can't be around you unless you do these things.

Love, Carla

Although Carla's father did not respond to her letter, she felt good that she had confronted him. Now she knew where he stood; she could go on with her life, instead of hoping things would change.

INDIRECT CONFRONTATIONS

If you cannot or do not wish to confront directly, you can opt for an indirect confrontation in which the person will have no knowledge of the confrontation. You can do this by role-playing, writing a letter, making a tape recording that you do not mail or deliver, or holding a fantasy confrontation.

Advantages. You are free to say what you need to without fearing their reaction. You can avoid getting personally involved, which can dredge up the drama and chaos all over again. You can maintain the safety of distance and still gain closure in the relationship.

Disadvantages. You may feel as if you "missed out" on having the chance to confront directly. You may continue to wonder what it would have felt like to speak your mind, to stand up to them once and for all.

For many people just the thought of confronting the perpetrator—even in a fantasy—is so frightening that it brings on a sort of paralysis. If the perpetrator was extremely abusive, you may still be intimidated by him. Even though he is no longer around or may even be dead, the *idea* of him may be so intense as to immobilize you. It is your inner child who is still afraid. The adult part of you will need to talk to your inner child and reassure her that you will not let anything happen to her. Listen to her fears; don't discount them. Allowing her to face her fears will make them less powerful.

Fantasy Confrontation

This visualization exercise can be used either as a practice confrontation or as an indirect way of confronting.

1. Lie down or sit in a comfortable position with pillows near you. Close your eyes, breathe deeply, and relax.
2. Visualize the person you need to confront. Visualize a safe place for the meeting. It could be your own home, or maybe you feel safer outdoors where there is lots of

space. Visualize the person approaching you before he or she sees you. Notice the facial expressions, the posture. When the person sees you, look for changes in facial expression and posture.

3. Sit down facing each other and begin your confrontation. You are going to speak; your confrontee will only listen, without making any comment. Try to speak out loud if you can, or just imagine what you would say. Remember to breathe deeply throughout the exercise.
4. After you have said all that you wish to say, rest quietly for a moment. Cry if you need to. If you wish, allow the other person to have a turn to speak. What do you imagine their response to be to what you have said?
5. If you are angered by the response or you don't agree with something that has been said, quietly begin saying no. Continue saying no until you can say it louder and louder. Yell, "No!" at each exhale of your breath, remembering to breathe deeply.
6. If you have built up a lot of anger and need to release it physically, place two pillows at your sides, under your fists. With each exhale, say, "No!" and come down hard with your fists on the pillows.
7. Allow any feelings or tears to come while you rest from the confrontation. When you get up, write down your experience if you choose. You may also want to share it with a supportive person.

Which form of confrontation to choose? *You* are the only one who can decide which is right for you. The important thing is that once you have confronted either directly or indirectly, you have taken a major step toward resolving the relationship. In the next chapter we will discuss making the decision to temporarily separate from, to permanently divorce from, or to reconcile with your parents, the perpetrator, and other members of your childhood family. Confronting makes this decision far easier.

STEP 4

Resolving Your Relationships

AFTER YOU HAVE confronted your childhood family with the truth and with your anger, some kind of *resolution* is called for so that you can go on with your life. At this point you will have to decide whether to continue seeing your parents, or whether it is best to take a break from them in order to work through the problems. You can resolve your relationships by any of three ways: (1) "trial" or temporary separation; (2) "divorce" or permanent separation; or (3) reconciliation.

It has been my experience that no matter what a survivor ultimately decides to do, many choose to have a temporary separation from their parents or other members of their childhood family *while* they are going through the recovery process. Even those who have seemingly good relationships with their childhood family find it difficult to be around them while they are recovering. It is a rare family who rallies around a survivor, providing her understanding and support. Most family members become defensive and angry when the silence is broken and the secret is revealed. Instead of offering support they often try to undermine the survivor's attempts at recovery. After the survivor becomes stronger and completes more of the recovery process, then she is better equipped to decide exactly which option she will ultimately take—to reconcile or to divorce. In the meantime, temporary separation may be the most practical option.

TRIAL OR TEMPORARY SEPARATION

If your progress toward recovery is thwarted each time you see your parents, if you revert to being a subservient or fearful child, then you may need to stop seeing them for a while. Most important, you may need time to develop your own separate self, since it may be impossible for you to maintain a sense of individuality when you are around them.

As Janet describes her situation, "I feel certain that the quality of my life would improve substantially if I didn't have to spend time with my parents. Each time I see them it's such an ordeal that it takes me weeks to recover. Afterward, I walk away not knowing who I am! Why do I put myself through it?"

Putting time and space between you and your parents may alleviate your having to contend with how they feel and with their criticism. Little progress may be made in your own recovery process if you only continue to repeat the same negative patterns of communication and behavior each time you get together. But time away may help you to distance yourself just enough to not get "hooked" back into these negative patterns. A trial separation may also help you to be more objective, to enable you to see their problems and manipulative ploys.

Although June's mother was constantly criticizing her (for being in therapy, for not forgetting the past, for not wanting to see her incestuous father), June couldn't stand up to her.

"I didn't want to hurt her, but I felt so angry. I just couldn't take care of myself when I was around her."

So June stopped seeing her mother for a year, during which time she received many letters either pleading for June to change her mind or accusing her of being an "ungrateful child." But June knew that if she were to get better she needed that distance until she could handle her mother's anger, criticism, and guilt. "Now, when I see her, I have more self-confidence. If she does something I don't like I can tell her about it. I've worked through my old anger toward her for not taking care of me as a child, and now I can take care of myself. Unlike before, I expect her to treat me with respect, and I let her know this loud and clear."

Your parents can also benefit from a trial separation—although this should *not* be your primary purpose for seeking it. This sort of parting gives them time to think things over and may even give them time to miss you enough to make some changes. Eva had tried unsuccessfully for a long time to get her parents to go into therapy with her, but after staying away for six months, she was surprised by their change of heart. "My parents said they would do anything to get me back. I agreed to see them again only if they would go into therapy with me. Through therapy, we are learning to communicate better. They listen to me less defensively, and they finally believe me about the abuse."

A trial separation will give you time to see how you really feel about your parents or family and will test out what it would be like to have a permanent separation. Your parents or family will be given another chance to treat you differently, and you, of course, will be able to ascertain whether you feel better or worse not being around them.

There is no prescribed or recommended amount of time necessary for you to spend away from your parents and no "best way" for you to schedule it. Some people stay away for only a few months, while others have stayed away for years.

You may decide to play it by ear, depending on how you feel at the time and how separate you become. Set up your "time away" in any way that feels right for you. You may choose to have a complete break with no communication at all, you may want to limit the time you spend with them, or you may choose to communicate with them only by mail or telephone.

Betty explained why she decided to have no contact. "I tried talking to them on the phone, but they'd start telling me I should stop therapy, forget the past, and go on. When I got off the phone I would doubt the whole recovery process. I just had to stop all contact with them for a while. I knew if I didn't, they would sabotage my recovery."

Some choose to limit their time with their family to important functions such as weddings, funerals, and anniversaries, or for the important holidays such as Christmas or birthdays. Still others limit their contact further to strictly "important news," communicated in letters and phone calls.

You will also need to decide how to tell your parents about your need for this time away. Some choose to confront their parents (in person, by mail, or on the phone) and tell them exactly why they don't wish to see them for a while. Tammy told her parents on the phone, "It slows down my recovery process when I see you. I need to take a vacation from you for a while so I can get better." Rosey told her parents in a letter, "I don't want to see you now and I don't know if I ever will. Maybe time away will help me feel better about you. I just don't know."

Others just avoid their parents and family and make up excuses as to why they can't see them. As Sandra relates, "Fortunately, I live far enough away from them so that my excuses are somewhat believable. I tell them I'm just too busy or I don't have the money."

Sometimes, after a trial separation, survivors decide to discontinue contact with their parents altogether. As Rene explains, "I hadn't really planned on a permanent separation, but after three months of not seeing them I felt so much better! Now I'm free, and I don't want to get trapped again."

DIVORCING YOUR PARENTS

None of us wants to come to the conclusion that we need to divorce ourself entirely from one or both of our parents. Instead, we usually hold on, hoping against hope that they will finally change. We stay tied to them by fooling ourselves into believing that there is a possibility of change when such a probability is minimal at best. You may have continued hoping that if you waited long enough, your parents would finally give you what you need. While reason may tell you that all that hoping is in vain—that your parents either don't have it to give or don't choose to—you may keep hoping just the same.

Perhaps the strongest reason for maintaining false hope is based on the great fear that you will be alone in the world. Even though you may be surrounded by a loving and caring spouse, children of your own, friends, your support group, and your therapist, your inner child may strongly resist cutting the cord. The child within has to be taught she *will* survive if she does not have her parents. She needs to overcome her fears of abandonment. This reassurance is essential if you finally realize you must give up hope. The price of continuing your relationship with your parents may be just too high.

Permanent separation is usually the only possible resolution if either parent does any of the following:

- Continues to abuse you either verbally, physically, emotionally, or sexually and you are unable to stand up for yourself.
- Continues to deny that you were sexually abused, persists in protecting the perpetrator, or blames you for the abuse.

- Continues to tell you that you are "insane" or irrational, thereby causing you to doubt your own sanity.
- Is the perpetrator and still denies the sexual abuse.
- Abuses your children or will not protect them from someone who is abusive.
- Either directly or indirectly brings you only pain when you get together.
- Is emotionally disturbed, a practicing alcoholic, or a drug abuser and refuses to get help.

The decision to "divorce" your parents may be your only alternative when the relationship is so destructive that you must choose between your health and them. Donna described her predicament: "My whole family is in quicksand. I'm trying to save them, but I'm going down with them in the process. I have to let go; it's either me or them."

One cautionary note: Don't stop seeing your parents in order to punish them. Any attempt on your part to blackmail them or seek revenge will backfire and probably cause further pain. The purpose of permanent disengagement is to protect yourself from further damage from them and to help facilitate your recovery.

Naturally, divorcing your parents will be very painful. Even those who haven't seen their parents in a long time have considerable difficulty when it comes to *permanently* severing the ties. If you are not already in therapy or in a support group, consider doing so before you attempt this momentous task. A good therapist can help you to become more clear about what the possible consequences are of breaking this primary relationship. He or she can also give you the added support you will need through this most difficult time.

Exercises for Saying Good-Bye

Saying good-bye usually takes place inside of you long before you actually act on it. Practicing saying good-bye can give you the courage to do it in person. It also helps you learn to say it in a way that will not show any confusion or wavering on your part. You can practice alone or in your support group, with a friend, or with your therapist.

1. Say out loud to your therapist or group what you would like to say to your parent or parents as a good-bye declaration. Get feedback as to how you sound. Have your therapist or a friend stand in for your parent, and then allow them to respond in the way they imagine your parent would, based on background information that you have provided.
2. Talk to an empty chair. When you feel you have said everything you want to say, get up and sit in that chair. Play the role of your parent, responding to what has just been said to you. Change chairs and roles as often as you feel you need to.
3. Have a fantasy confrontation in preparation for the real one. You can do this exercise as a visualization (similar to the fantasy confrontation in the previous chapter) or as a writing exercise:
   - Get as comfortable as possible, preferably lying down on your back. Close your eyes and begin to breathe deeply. Imagine that you are going to see someone for the last time and picture a comfortable, safe place in which to meet. Take a look around. Notice the details (the furniture, the landscape).
   - Watch the person approaching you. (He or she hasn't seen you yet.) Notice the facial expression and posture. Now you are recognized. Notice the facial ex-

pression and posture once again. Did either change once you were noticed?

- Sit down together to talk. What will you say to this person, since it will be your last encounter?
- Say out loud, "Good-bye." Repeat it over and over, saying it louder as you go along. Watch the person walk away. If you have been able to let go of the person, pay attention to how you now feel. If you can't say good-bye, what is standing in the way of your letting go?

4. If it turns out that you are not ready to say good-bye, that's okay. When you are ready, you will be able to do it. Note your reasons for holding on, and see if you can work with your resistance.

These practice sessions may help ready you to say good-bye to your parent or parents. On the other hand, they may show you that you are unable to make a complete break. If this is the case, you may decide to try to restrict the relationship a little at a time, instead of making a permanent separation all at once. It may be helpful to take longer "vacations" from them, seeing them only infrequently. Or you may want to end certain aspects of the relationship, such as not talking on the phone with them every day or every week. These weaning techniques can help you to experience your fears in small doses and to calm the frightened child in you. During this time, it will also help to call on friends and other "support" people for reassurance that you are not all alone. This will be the time when you redirect your energies from your parents to other more fruitful pursuits.

If, on the other hand, a final break seems inevitable, you may want some formal, personal closure. Consider the formal declaration of divorce that Connie wrote, which you can, of course, tailor to suit yourself:

Declaration of Divorce

I, ______, being of sound mind and body, do hereby claim Final Judgment of Dissolution from ______, parents of said Petitioner.

The Petitioner, ______, claims as causes, unusual punishment and cruel and malicious treatment from the named offenders. Let it be known that as of ______, ______ claims no relation to all above-named offenders. The Petitioner is under no obligation financially or emotionally to any of the above offenders. The Petitioner, ______, is granted status as a single person with no immediate relatives. Therefore, the Petitioner, ______, claims no relationship at all to the above offenders.

Here is the letter Sharon wrote to her mother:

Dear Mom,

This is to let you know that we can no longer be mother and daughter. I tried to talk with you at my therapist's office about the rapes and the effects they have had on me. You said I was crazy to make such a big deal out of this. You said I should just *forget it.* Well, maybe you can forget it, but I can't. It has affected my whole life and in a sense has made it a disaster.

Now that I have brought it out in the open, you have refused the help and love I need (as you did when I was a child). Well, I am no longer a child. I am 39 years old. A part of me still loves you and needs you, but I can honestly say that I don't want you as a mother, because you can't be what I need or want. This hurts me as much as it will hurt you, but I must face the fact that you won't be there for me. I guess I have hoped for that for too long, and it just never came true. Good-bye.

You may decide to divorce your parents in person. In this case, refer to the confrontation preparation exercise described earlier. If you have been able to successfully complete this exercise, you are probably ready for a real face-to-face good-bye. As you did in the exercise, choose a safe place for your meeting. Know what you are going to say ahead of time, and make sure you say everything you want to say. There is no need for discussion; just say your good-byes, and leave.

Comforting Your Inner Child

Divorcing your parents can be a wrenching experience. Even though the adult part of you may know that on an intellectual, logical level you must let them go, your child will still feel emotionally abandoned. As a result, your inner child will need your care now more than ever. She doesn't know that she doesn't need those parents anymore. All she needs is you. But she cannot let go of them if you don't give her the nurturing and parenting she needs.

The following exercise will help you to stay in touch with your inner child during this time of grieving:

1. Lie down on your bed or couch and breathe deeply. Try to get your body as relaxed and comfortable as possible.
2. Imagine you are hearing a child crying. This is your inner child. Imagine going over to her and asking why she is crying. What does she say?
3. Imagine you are able to comfort her in some way. What would you do? What would you say?
4. Stay with your inner child until she feels safe. Listen to what she has to say. Tell her whatever you feel she needs in order to feel comforted.

Often, as with any type of "divorce," you may still need to have occasional contact with your parents. Perhaps you want your children to have access to their grandparents. (Remember, however, that if your parents were abusive to you, they may very well be abusive to your children.) Or you may wish to attend family gatherings, weddings, graduations, or funerals. You may choose to risk facing your parents in order to attend an event that concerns someone you love. Lisa anguished over going to her niece's wedding: "I played it through in my mind dozens of times. I didn't think I could go through with it. But just before the wedding I decided to go, because I wanted to be there for my niece. I took a friend for moral support, and we didn't sit with the family. I saw my parents, and that was pretty upsetting, but at least I didn't have to talk to them."

You may also be caught off guard by unexpected contact with your parents. If you accidentally run into them or happen to answer the phone when they call (perhaps to speak to your children or to discuss some sort of "business"), you may feel as if someone punched you in the stomach. An associate of mine describes the phenomenon as a "mother wallop" (since it seems to occur most often and most intensely in response to contact with mothers).

If you get hit with a "mother wallop" and it sends you reeling, don't be overly concerned. You *will* recover from it. Give yourself time to let your confidence return before you "go another round" with your parents. You may need to comfort yourself. Hug your stuffed animal, go to bed and wrap yourself in soft sheets or blankets. Just as you need to stay off or rest an injured leg or arm, rest your emotionally wounded body for a while. Give yourself time to heal. Your parents will not always have this power over you. They may have won this round, but they haven't won the fight.

Reconsidering the Divorce

It is not uncommon for a client who has just heard from a "divorced" parent to suddenly start doubting herself. The incessant internal questioning takes over: "Maybe I am being unfair, maybe they have changed; perhaps I should give them another chance." Just one contact can reactivate a flood of feelings held in check for months. For others, just one unplanned contact with parents may convince them to resume the lapsed relationship. If you do find yourself longing for such a resumption, remember these things:

- It is usually not our love that keeps us tied to our parents; it is our illness.
- Our attempt to reconcile with our parents may be just an avoidance of our pain, our loneliness, or our need for more work on ourselves.
- Our need to be "fair" and "balanced" is sometimes so extreme it may border on sickness.
- If our parents could not love and appreciate us when we were adorable little children, how are they going to be able to love us as adults?

Even if you never have occasion to see or hear from your parents again, you will not, of course, be able to totally block them out of your mind. They will always be a part of your life. There will naturally be things that remind you of them, and you will probably always have an empty place in your heart for them. But sometimes we need to protect our hearts so they can have a chance to heal—so that we can be free to love ourselves and others.

Not all divorces involve a *physical* cutting of all ties. Some survivors continue to see their parents occasionally, but they consider themselves "emotionally divorced" from them. An emotional divorce is an abandonment of any further attempts to change your parents or have a close bond with them. One may be physically present, but one is emotionally absent.

RECONCILIATION

If you can retain your sense of self in your family relationship, and if the relationship changes in ways that are healthy for you, reconciliation can be a way to experience whatever love has survived. The main question you must ask yourself is, Do I see any signs, however small, of some *consistent* progress on the part of my parent? Don't expect changes to occur right away. Remember how long it has taken you to be able to make your own changes. And don't expect the changes to be major. Look for small indications from them at first, such as less defensiveness when you talk to them about the sexual abuse.

No matter what your parents have done, you probably still love them and want whatever love they can still give you. You therefore may decide that it is too painful for you to live your life without them. Before you attempt a reconciliation, however, make certain that you can take care of yourself around them. You have changed, but they may not have. Even if they have changed in some ways, they may still talk to you and treat you in the same abusive, negative, or "crazy-making" ways as before. Wishful thinking can cause you to see changes where there are none. Above all, don't allow them to abuse you in any way.

The following suggestions will help you make the most of your reconciliation efforts:

1. Make sure you can be with your parents and still take care of yourself emotionally and psychologically. Take responsibility for the frequency and circumstances of the visits. Consider the following:

   - Seeing your parents less often, or for shorter periods of time.
   - Seeing them only when there are others present—or the reverse, seeing them only when you can be alone with them.
   - Working at communicating your needs better, such as saying no when you do not want to do something.
2. Be realistic; do not expect it to be easy. Have reasonable expectations of the relationship. Everything will not all be different and wonderful.
3. Make sure you have a plan of action. Do not expect things to just "work out" without effort on both your parts.
   - Set regular time aside for family members to "hash out" problems.
   - *Actively* work on learning to communicate effectively with one another. Ask your parent(s) or other family members to go into therapy with you. Read some of the popular books on good communication within families.
   - Recommend that your parents read this and other books on childhood sexual abuse so they can better understand what you are going through.
4. As with all reconciliations, you and your parents need to make a *mutual agreement* to "bury the hatchet" and go on. Your agreement might include the following joint commitments:
   - We will talk things out, look for solutions, and seek outside help when needed.
   - We agree to *listen* to one another.
   - We agree to stop *blaming* one another, although it is okay to to express anger. We will also try to explain why we are angry.

Sit down with your parents and family and discuss what

your "peace treaty" will include. Make suggestions, but also listen to what they feel they need. Spend time alone deciding what *you* need as a part of the peace treaty. Vicki, for example, who had been molested by her older brother, Doug, presented her parents with this statement when she was still "negotiating" the relationship:

> If I am going to be able to have a meaningful relationship with you I will need the following from you:
>
> I need to talk about the abuse and how I feel about it.
>
> I want nothing to do with Doug. I refuse to be in the same house with him, so stop trying to "bring the family together." I am not going to ever see him, and I am not going to change my mind about it.
>
> I do not want any of my children to ever be around Doug. If you don't agree to this I will have to keep the kids away from you.

Vicki's parents agreed to her terms and then told her what they in turn expected:

> We will listen to you about how the abuse affected you for as long as we can. Sometimes it makes us feel so terrible we can't listen very long.
>
> We understand that you are angry, but we don't want to have to hear you complaining to us about it all the time.
>
> We will not allow Doug to be around Ricky and Lisa, but we love him and consider him a part of the family no matter what he has done.

Vicki could agree with the first two requirements, but she had a hard time accepting the fact that her parents still chose to be around her brother. Once again, it seemed they were choosing Doug over her. But after she thought about it, she decided that if they were willing to meet all her terms, she would stop trying to make them choose between her and Doug. Vicki was ready to reconcile.

During this process, you may come to realize that you are not ready for a cease-fire—your anger may still be so intense that all you want to do is let out your rage at them. You may need to spend more time releasing your anger in constructive ways, working on your problems in therapy or in a support group. Your parents may need to do the same. (Parents United has groups for perpetrators and silent partners.)

WHAT ABOUT FORGIVENESS?

You may have noticed that nowhere so far has anything been said about forgiveness. There is a difference between forgiveness and reconciliation. You may not be ready or able to forgive by the time you are ready to attempt a reconciliation. Perhaps during the reconciliation process itself you will obtain enough trust and healing to be able to forgive.

Others will try to make you feel guilty for not forgiving. But sometimes choosing *not* to forgive can actually help in the recovery process. Many survivors purposefully do not forgive in order to maintain distance from their parents. As Marsha explained, "When I was growing up, my father would beg me to forgive him after each time he molested me. I'd feel guilty for not forgiving him, so eventually I would tell him I had. Then he would sexually abuse me again. I felt tricked and humiliated. Now I protect myself from being his victim all over again by *not* forgiving him."

For some survivors, it is actually harder to withhold forgiveness than it is to forgive. They have a tendency to forgive too quickly and fail to consider their own needs. Attempting to forgive your parents can sometimes be a way of pleasing them and neglecting yourself. It is much harder to express your anger and openly acknowledge what your parents have done to hurt you than it is to minimize it and forgive and forget. Once you have acknowledged and released your anger, you will be in a much better position to forgive.

Victims often want to be "good" and "fair": "If I don't forgive I'll be just like *them;* I'll be on their level." Forgiving and thus being "good" carries the illusion of compensating for the victim's sense of "badness." Other people have the fantasy that everything will be okay if they just forgive. "I thought I could take away all the pain if I forgave my parents. It didn't work; the pain is still there."

If you want to forgive, ask yourself what your reasons are for doing so. You may be sacrificing yourself once again, or setting yourself up to be revictimized. True forgiveness comes as a by-product of recovery. As you become better able to take care of yourself, you may feel more forgiving of those who have hurt you.

On the other hand, some survivors have found a way of forgiving their parents because of their strong religious beliefs, but they cannot reconcile with them. As Judy explained, "I was able to forgive my father for sexually abusing me because God teaches us to forgive. I don't blame my father anymore, but I still hold him accountable for his actions. I can forgive him because he is human and therefore fallible, but I still don't want to be around him."

You can recover and resolve your relationships without forgiving others. Forgiveness is not a voluntary act but is something that may or may not spontaneously occur as part of the recovery process.

LETTING GO

Whether you have a trial separation, "divorce" your parents, or reconcile with them, you will undoubtedly experience a feeling of tremendous loss. Even a reconciliation involves letting go of familiar, negative patterns of relating to your parents, which can also be difficult. What else are you letting go of?

- Fantasies of finally getting what you missed as a child.
- Your illusions about your parents.
- Trying to change your parents.
- Trying to please your parents.

These changes, while extremely positive, will nevertheless take some getting used to. If you feel like grieving because relationships have changed or terminated, this is normal and natural. The places that held the pain, the anger, the illusions, and the problems may now seem empty. But you will now be able to fill up those empty places with positive feelings, reality, and a more fulfilling life.

New Beginnings

1. Prepare for this visualization exercise by getting comfortable and deep-breathing. Now, close your eyes and relax. Visualize your inner child. Imagine that you are taking her for a walk by the ocean, or in a forest or a desert—wherever you'd like. As you walk along, notice the landscape around you, the smells, the sounds.
2. Even though you are outdoors, you come upon a large, open door. Through this door streams a beautiful white light. Walk with your inner child through this open door. What do you see? What lies ahead for you and your inner child?
3. Open your eyes. Write down your thoughts.

You and your inner child can have a new beginning. Walk through the open door. There really is a whole other world out there.

STEP 5

Self-Discovery

WHETHER YOU TEMPORARILY separate, "divorce," or reconcile with your parents, you will need to start developing your own separate identity. It's time to be your own person, with your own values, beliefs, priorities, and feelings. You will always be influenced by your parents, of course, but you need to decide which of their values and beliefs you want to accept and which ones you don't. Otherwise, you will identify with the totality of them, and you may end up being just like them. If you see that you have a tendency to be like your parents in a particularly negative way (such as being abusive to others), you will need to take a firm stand against their ways in order to be truly different from them.

Those who were sexually abused seldom have a strong sense of themselves. Unfortunately, you cannot separate completely and stand alone until you have established within yourself a sense of selfness, a sense of who *you* are, incorporating your values and your likes and dislikes. This core of self cannot be taken away from you. Through self-awareness and self-knowledge, you will establish a mental image of your own identity.

Many people define themselves in terms of the roles they play in life. They are the children of their parents, the wives or husbands of their spouses, the parents of their children; they are teachers, salespeople, homemakers, employees, employers. But the self is more than the roles the self plays.

Who Are You?

Without taking time to think about it, spontaneously complete the following sentence in four different ways:

I am . . .

See how many of your responses describe roles that you play. These are the outer part of you, a secondary part that often changes with time and experience. The roles you play in personal and work relationships are an important part of existence, but your identity goes deeper to a you that is constant.

Next, complete the following sentence describing your *qualities* ("determined," "capable," "independent") or describe your *feelings* ("joyous," "afraid," "angry") in four ways:

I am . . .

Review the sentences you just composed. Realize that recognizing your own characteristics is part of identifying yourself. You know more about you than anyone else.

An important aspect of discovering yourself is learning the difference between you and your parents. List the major characteristics of the following people, regardless of whether you consider these traits good or bad:

My mother is (was) . . .
My father is (was) . . .
My (other primary caretaker) is (was) . . .
I am . . .

HOW YOUR SELF WAS FORMED

Look at the lists you have made, and you will see that you share some characteristics with the people who reared you. You probably took on those characteristics because you admired those traits or because you believed those traits would help you, but this is not always the case. Sometimes we identify through a process of elimination. You may have looked at one parent and said to yourself, "I'll never be like him," and instead looked for other role models. Unfortunately, if you were exposed to only a few people (as is the case for many survivors who were isolated from others), your only other significant role model may have been your other parent. Although you may not have wanted to be like that parent either, believing your choices were limited to just those two, you chose the lesser of two evils.

You may have also identified with those you are angry with or afraid of. This is called *identifying with the aggressor.* Hoping to gain their power and thus defend yourself against the danger they represent, you may have tried to resemble those you fear or hate. In this way, then, in an unconscious attempt to subdue your feelings of helplessness and hopelessness, your abused inner child may have evolved to become a child abuser.

You may have decided very early on that you would never be like your weaker parent. This was Lynn's experience: "My mother is so passive, she lets my father abuse her and never says a thing. My father, on the other hand, never lets anyone walk over him!"

Sometimes our lives are dictated just as much by our attempts to *not* be like one of our parents as they are to be like them. If you notice in yourself behavior that you do not like, ask yourself, "Am I behaving this way because I don't want to be like my parent?" or "Am I acting like one parent as some kind of protection from or guarantee that I won't be like the other parent?"

Melissa's parents were extremely rigid and strict. Everything had to be done just a certain way or they would punish her severely. Her room had to be immaculate, her clothes had to be pressed perfectly, her school papers could not have any erasures. As an adult, Melissa is just the opposite of her parents. She is extremely disorganized and undisciplined. "I want to have more control over my life, but every time I start to get organized I think I'm becoming like my parents. I hate my life the way it is, but I just can't risk ending up like them," she says. By making sure she was *not* like her parents, Melissa did not leave much room to discover *herself.* You are just as bound to your parents if you choose to be completely opposite of them as when you decide to be a carbon copy of them. Neither choice allows you much self-discovery.

Refer back to the lists you made describing your parents' characteristics. Circle those good qualities in your parents that you have identified with. Draw a box around those "bad" qualities that you have either identified with or modified to some extent. Of those negative qualities you have taken on, think of ways that you can modify your behavior to avoid being a replica of that parent.

Now ask yourself how you are *different* from your parents. List all the ways. Why do you think you developed these qualities?

Even though you identified with your parents and took on many of their characteristics, *you are not them.* You do not have to make the same mistakes they made. For example, you do not have to be either passive and dependent like your mother or abusive and angry like your father. There is an in-between, a middle ground, a balance. Most important, you do not need to "pass on" the family legacy of abuse. The cycle of abuse can stop with you.

Recalling Your Childhood

What about the other important people in your life? There undoubtedly were people who influenced you, with whom you identified out of love and admiration: teachers, friends, movie stars, characters in books, neighbors, baby-sitters, and other members of your family. Make a list of all the people who stand out in your mind as being important to you during your childhood. Try to recall one person from your childhood who showed you some caring and kindness. Close your eyes and visualize how this person looked, what he or she did or said. There may be one particular incident that stands out in your mind. Visualize this incident. Remember how it felt to have someone care.

Open your eyes and write about your visualization. How did you feel about this person? How did this person affect your life? Make a list describing his or her personal qualities and how you were treated.

Example: "The nice lady" (you may not even know her name) . . .

was kind to me.
treated me like I was important, like I had value.
was generous.
was independent, traveled a lot, was an adventurer.

Describe how each quality affected you and influenced your personality.

Example:

> "No one had ever been kind like that. It made me feel good about myself. I try to be kind like her. I try to spend time with people who are lonely or uncared for. This has influenced my career choice."

Actively seek more positive role models now. Your personality is still being affected by others, so seek new models to replace the old. You are not going to *become* these people; rather, you are going to be opening your horizons and expanding your awareness and options. You had so few positive role models as a child. Give yourself now what you never had.

PARENTAL MESSAGES

As a child, you were repeatedly bombarded with messages from your parents about who you were. These messages were both spoken and unspoken (facial expressions, tone of voice). For example, if your parents told you that you were pretty, smart, and lovable, the chances are very high that you developed a positive self-image. But if they told you that you were ugly, stupid, and selfish, the reverse probably occurred—you believed them, and your self-image plummeted.

Negative Messages

Write down all the negative messages you received about yourself from your parents and family of origin.

1. Being as objective as you can, decide which messages are true and which are false.
2. Cross out all the negative messages on the list that you no longer believe.
3. Circle those messages that you still believe to be true.

Of those that you believe are true today, which are really *negative?* Rachel's parents, for example, would tell her, "You are so stubborn and pigheaded." But what her parents described as being "stubborn" was her unwillingness to allow them to run her life—and many people do not necessarily consider that quality negative; rather, they describe such behavior as assertive. So just because your parents consider one of your qualities negative does not make it so. Before you decide that a negative message is true, consult with someone whose opinion you value greatly—or, better yet, consult with several people. Sometimes we are so brainwashed by the negative messages we received in our upbringing that we cannot see ourselves with unjaundiced eyes.

If you do believe that your parents' messages are correct and true, that you do have many negative qualities, understand that you do not have to continue owning them. You *can* change. In fact, you have already taken the steps toward changing by acknowledging what you already have to yourself.

THE POWER OF POSITIVE THOUGHT

Negatives and Positives

Make a list of all your "negative" qualities, all your shortcomings and weaknesses, all the things you do not like about yourself. Then list all the positive strengths, attributes, and things you do like about yourself.

Which list is longer? If your negatives list is longer than your positives, maybe you tend to focus more on your liabilities than your assets. Do you take your strengths and positive attributes for granted but concentrate instead on your weaknesses? If you look for the negative, you will always find it. Besides, you may have had alot more practice finding the negatives because that is what your parents practiced on you.

Be advised: *Do not continue treating yourself the way your parents treated you!* Give yourself permission to see what is *right* with you. Since you probably believe in fairness, start by focusing on your assets at *least* as often as you do your liabilities. You don't have to sweep your weaknesses under the carpet, but try to balance them with your positives. *Be fair to yourself.*

If your weaknesses list is considerably longer than your strengths list, ask a supportive friend who knows you well for help in adding to your strengths list. Carry this strengths list around to add to whenever you think of something new or when someone gives you praise. Continue this process until your strengths list is at least as long as your weaknesses list.

Read over your strengths list at least once a week. As you go over each strength, take a deep breath and along with it the knowledge that you possess this positive quality. You cannot hold onto your negative self-image if you let in evidence of your positive attributes.

Work on countering the negative messages with positive statements (see table).

Example of Changing Negatives into Positives

I am *(list your negative)*	*(Change it into a positive)*
angry.	I'm angry and that's okay.
spaced out.	I'm getting less and less spaced out every day.
passive.	It's healthy to assert my rights.
uncommunicative.	I have the right to ask for what I want and to say how I feel.

Not only do our parents give us negative messages about ourselves, but they also teach us to discount, dismiss, and disown certain natural aspects of ourselves. They did this by teaching us "commandments" that cripple our ability to love ourselves and others. Those who were sexually abused were often taught the following list of powerful commandments. Add to the list any of your own that are not mentioned.

Don't trust others.
Don't tell others about what goes on in the family.
Don't feel [whatever it was they didn't approve of].
Don't question authority.
Don't listen to or respect your body.
Don't get angry or assert yourself.
Don't think for yourself.
Don't reveal yourself.
Don't take care of yourself.
Don't ask for help.

Consciously challenge each commandment that you no longer believe. Ask yourself what price you continue to pay for believing and following it. Do you seriously want to pay that price? Give yourself permission to discard those commandments that are preventing you from being the you that you want to be. Sift through all the beliefs and messages you were given by your parents and significant others and decide which you will keep and which you will discard. *All* your parents' ideas, beliefs, and values were not false or dysfunctional; indeed, some may have been practical and valuable. Decide for yourself which ones to believe, which are true for you.

In some ways, it may feel like you are starting over—and in many ways you will be. You will be giving up old defenses, old beliefs, and old ways of coping. In place of these negative attitudes and beliefs, you will instill positive messages. You can do this through the use of affirmations (positive, life-affirming statements) such as:

I am my own person.
I am separate and different from my parents/my siblings.
I deserve to have a life separate and different from my parent(s).
I am a unique individual.

Pay attention to what you are *thinking.* Are your thoughts during the day mostly negative messages to yourself? Pay attention to your *self-talk.* Are you giving yourself the same critical messages you got from your family? These negative messages only act as a deterrent to your recovery. Try to catch yourself whenever you engage in a critical, negative thought about yourself and *stop it!* Find out where you got that message. Whose voice is it you are hearing—your own, or one of your parents'? Counter the message with something like "That's not true! I am *not* stupid. I just made a common mistake." Then work on replacing your negative self-talk with positive affirmations, such as "I am a special person" or "I am intelligent."

YOUR EMOTIONS—THE KEY TO THE SELF

One of the best ways to discover who you are is to focus on what you feel. Our emotions are the key that unlocks the door to ourselves. Only by knowing yourself through your emotions can you grow to truly trust yourself, your perceptions, and your thoughts.

An integral part of your "self" is your particular emotion at any given moment. Unfortunately, you have probably come to seldom focus attention on how you feel. Start now. Begin by spending at least five minutes a day "checking yourself out" and asking the following questions:

How am I feeling right now?

What emotions am I feeling today?
Why am I feeling this emotion? What caused it?

To discover how you are feeling, pay attention to how your *body* feels. Do you have tension or pain anywhere? Do you know what is causing this discomfort? What emotion do you associate with the discomfort? Fear? Anger? Sadness? Getting in touch with your body will help you to get in touch with your emotions.

Continue this self-discovery process periodically throughout the day. A good time to discover how you are feeling is early in the morning, when we tend to be more open and vulnerable, before we put up our walls in order to face the world. Sit quietly, breathe deeply, and just see what feelings emerge. At this time you may remember a dream. In your dreams you can express feelings that you may be afraid to confront when you are awake.

Take a walk in the early morning or after you get home in the evening. Use this time to get to know your emotions better. You can even express some emotions as you walk, telling someone off in your mind, stomping on them with each step. Give yourself permission to express any and all of your emotions. Each time you deny a feeling, you deny a part of your *self.* Express your fear, your hurt, your anger, and your joy. Each time you hide your feelings, you alienate yourself not only from others but from your *self.*

OPENING UP YOUR SENSES

Sexually abused people tend to shut down their senses in much the same way as they close off their emotions. The sensation overload that occurred during the abuse may have been too much for a young child's system to bear. And so, during the abuse you stopped *seeing* so as not to be part of what the perpetrator was doing to you, so as not to see his sexual organs, and so as not to have to feel. You stopped *hearing* as a way of drowning out the sounds of panting, moaning, and sexual words. You stopped *smelling* to block out the dirty sheets, body odor, or alcohol breath. You stopped *tasting* so as not to taste ejaculate, the taste of genitals, the taste of the abuser's mouth. You blocked out your ability to *feel* in order to protect yourself from the agonizing pain of penetration, the betrayal of your body if it started to feel aroused, the pain of being held down, smothered, or thrown across the room.

Now it is time to allow those sensations to return—not in flashbacks or as a way of bringing back the memories, but in order to reconnect with yourself and the world in positive ways. There is a beautiful world out there. It is time to rediscover it, and yourself in the process. There is a world of sights, sounds, smells, tastes, and touches that can bring you back to life. Allow your ears to hear all the sounds of your environment. Open yourself up to the beauty of music. Allow yourself the sensation of touch. Begin to explore your environment just by touching it. Rediscover how it feels to be touched, how it feels to touch another person. Try especially to open your eyes wider, to see more clearly. Really *look* at your surroundings instead of seeing them in a haze. Instead of walking around with "tunnel vision," sharpen your awareness of the periphery as well.

When talking to someone, try to really *see* who it is. Notice the details of her features, what he is wearing, how she is sitting or standing. Notice the color of his eyes. Notice the shades and nuances of color all around you. Absorb the sight of the foliage around you. Compare colors. Is that shade of green darker than the other shade of green? Does it have more blue in it or more yellow?

Your world and the way you sense and perceive it is a part of you. Notice how you are affected by your physical environment. Are you happier on sunny days or cloudy ones? Do you prefer summer or winter, spring or fall? Which do you like better, the daytime or the nighttime? When are you most alert? Do you prefer the seaside, the mountains, or the desert? Which environment helps you to get the most in touch with yourself and your feelings?

Learn about yourself by discovering your preferences. What is your favorite color? What type of music do you prefer? What is your favorite smell? Your favorite food? Your favorite thing to touch? Where do you like to be touched and how? Start asking yourself all sorts of questions like this; you'll deepen your awareness of how your environment affects you and who you are.

KEEPING A JOURNAL

Start a journal of your thoughts, feelings, and sensations. At first, don't write about others at all (how you feel about someone else, how you perceive someone else). The only person to write about is you. Later you can include how you relate to others and how you are affected by others. But for now, stick to writing about how you perceive yourself and how you feel about yourself. Include your feelings about your activities, your goals, your dreams, and your life. Keep writing until you have a solid sense of yourself.

Through journal keeping, you can discover more about yourself than you ever imagined possible. You will discover thoughts and feelings long buried, and you will discover the reasons for them. Writing can also help you to discover solutions and alternatives, new ways of looking at things, and most important, new ways of looking at yourself.

To help you focus on yourself in the journal, start each entry with the following constructions:

Today I feel (felt) . . .

Today I think (thought) . . .
Today I noticed, saw, perceived . . .

Discovering yourself is the way toward recovery. Remember always that your self is made up of your thoughts, your feelings, and your sensations. Observing and paying attention to these will enrich your self-knowledge more than anything else will. As Pia experienced, "I am comfortable with *myself* for the first time in my life. I live in the *now.* I look around as I walk, noticing the sky, the flowers, the trees. I am no longer always worrying about my family. The dark clouds have lifted. I don't feel afraid anymore. I feel free."

STEP 6

Self-Care

YOU ARE NOT your parents. You do not have to act like them, and you do not have to treat *yourself* the way they treated you.

In dysfunctional families, parents seldom teach their children to take care of themselves. Neither by example nor by teaching did your parents show you how to properly attend to your own needs. As a child, if you took your needs to your parents (including your need for them to stop the sexual abuse), you were often ignored and rejected. Because of this you learned to hold back your needs in the same way you learned to hold back your feelings. Ironically, you were more likely to be the one to take care of your parents' needs.

Now it is time to acknowledge how very important your needs are and how important *you* are. Because you are letting go of so much (your dependence on your parents, your old negative beliefs), you will need to replace these negative things with healthier ideas, beliefs, and habits. Most important, you will need to learn self-care. This means doing some things you may not be used to doing:

Putting your own needs first.
Valuing and respecting yourself.
Praising and nurturing yourself.
Asking for what you want and saying no to what you don't want.
Recognizing that you have choices and rights.
Having privacy and time alone.
Doing only what you want with your body.
Expressing your feelings, opinions, and needs.
Making your own decisions.
Trusting yourself.

Like most survivors, you probably tend to be the care-giver rather than the care-receiver. Survivors tend to be good at being spouses and parents, anticipating their loved ones' needs, going the second mile when it comes to self-sacrifice. But seldom can they ask their loved ones to give to them. They fool themselves into thinking they don't need much (they got used to having very little as children), and they don't believe anyone would want to give to them even if they did ask. Survivors tend to be martyrs, sacrificing their own needs but expecting to be appreciated and revered for their unselfish, generous natures.

Does this sound like you? Have you spoiled those around you, leading them to believe that you have no needs? When you do ask for something, do you expect people to trip over themselves giving it to you because you ask for something so seldom? When people do not give "on demand," do you use this to validate your belief that "no one cares"?

When they are not in a relationship, survivors often do a better job of taking care of themselves. Rita experienced this phenomenon: "Before I met Robert, I was going to school at night, I was exercising, and I was eating right. Now I drag myself home at night, too tired to go to school or to exercise, and all I do is eat and take care of his needs." This is typical.

Many survivors tend to stop doing those things that gave them pleasure or a sense of accomplishment when they enter into a relationship and take on the task of pleasing their partner. It is not coincidence that many survivors gain weight when they are in a relationship. This is not because they are so "content and happy," but because they have stopped meeting their own needs. They don't know how to have a relationship and maintain a sense of themselves at the same time.

Survivors even choose jobs and professions in which they are the care-giver. As noted in a previous chapter, a large percentage of children who were sexually victimized grow up to become teachers, nurses, doctors, social workers, and therapists—any profession in which they can give to others or "rescue." Even as children, many took on the role of care-giver in the family. "Doing good" may have helped them to stop feeling quite so *bad* about themselves. Do you fit this pattern? Do you give to others what you never got? More important, do you give to others what you fail to give yourself? This is a very easy trap to fall into. All too often, a survivor gives so much of herself to others that she has nothing left for herself and even loses touch with the fact that she also has needs.

In addition to choosing care-giving professions, many survivors end up in positions of authority. This almost compulsive need to keep a tight rein on their environment comes not so much out of a need to control others but more from a need to *not* be controlled. From that out-of-control childhood, they vow to "never again" take orders from anyone. Unfortunately, this need to control what happens can end up ruling their life. In the end, they feel isolated and lonely, since their true needs are not being met at all. Have you allowed your need to be in control to interfere with your other needs? Have you hidden your real needs behind the cloak of authority?

Learning to take care of yourself will not be easy. Like many survivors, you were not taught how to take care of yourself, nor were you encouraged when you did. You probably often heard statements like "Stop thinking of yourself all the time!" or "Your poor mother works hard all day; why don't you help her more!" Your parents may also have given you certain nonverbal messages, indicating such things as "I can't meet your needs, I have too many of my own" or "I didn't get my needs met when I was a child, so you have to take care of me now." Consequently, you learned to sacrifice yourself for the sake of others. This made you easy prey to the child molester. You may have been told by the perpetrator that his needs were greater than yours, or that if you didn't cooperate, it would be the end of the family—and so you sacrificed.

Because of all this prior conditioning, you may still think that taking care of yourself is a very selfish act. "After all, if we all thought of just ourselves, what kind of a world would this be?" you might say. The answer is, probably not such a bad one, if we all *truly* took care of ourselves. Self-care makes it possible for you to truly care for others, not because you are vicariously living through them, not because you want to feel like a "good" person, but because you really *want* to. When you take care of your own needs first, when you value yourself and nurture yourself, you will feel good about yourself, and this love of self will spontaneously flow out of you to others.

It is only when we feel *deprived* that we resent giving to others. Self-care does not mean you stop caring about others; it just means you *start caring more about you.* As a survivor of sexual abuse, you probably have such an underdeveloped sense of your personal needs and rights that the last thing you need to worry about is becoming selfish.

Start by thinking about yourself more and others less. Make sure you aren't focusing all your energies outward. Since you have a *choice* between taking care of someone else or giving to yourself, try choosing yourself sometimes. At first this may be uncomfortable. You may feel guilty or selfish. You may be afraid that others won't like you unless you go along with what they want. But keep trying. Eventually you will find that nothing bad happens just because you do what you want to do at times. You can still meet others' needs. People may even like the new you better, since no one is really comfortable around a martyr.

LEARNING TO ASK FOR WHAT YOU WANT

Taking care of yourself also includes learning to ask for what you want and need from others, instead of waiting and hoping they will *notice* that you need something. Tell people what you want. Do not expect them to be mind readers. It is self-defeating to continue to think, "If he loved me enough, he'd *know* what I want," or "If I have to ask for it, I don't want it." That is the way a victim or martyr thinks, not a survivor. Survivors go after what they want and do not simply wait around for "handouts."

Survivors often think that "taking care of yourself" means that you must rely only on yourself to meet your own needs. But on the contrary, it also means beginning to reach out for help instead of always doing everything yourself (and then resenting it). Ask those you love and trust to assist you with the stresses and pressures of life when you feel overwhelmed. Do not continue to insist on always taking care of things yourself instead of admitting when you need help.

You may still be operating from the belief that you must do everything on your own because no one will ever be there for you. Or you may think that if you never speak up, you'll avoid the risk of rejection. Both these fears come from your childhood but no longer apply to you today as an adult. If you never reach out for help, you will continue to deprive yourself. If you continue to take care of everyone and everything yourself, you will not only be very lonely but will continue to be a victim and martyr.

As a child you received messages from your family to keep your mouth shut and remain *invisible.* You were invisible to your parents if they didn't want to see you, or if they were angry with you, or if they didn't want to see what was happening to you (the sexual abuse, for example). You also learned to become "invisible" in order to protect yourself. Well, you no longer need to be invisible to survive. If people do not notice you, they may not abuse you, but they also will not love you or attend to your needs. Make yourself and your needs known.

DON'T EXPECT OTHERS TO TAKE CARE OF YOU

Although you have a right to ask for what you want and need, do not make the mistake of *expecting* people to meet your needs just because you ask. Do not grow to *depend* on others to meet your needs. People who are well balanced ask for what they want but don't need to get all their needs met by other people. They know that they have a resource within that enables them to give to themselves. Victims do not know that. They do not realize that they *can* take care of themselves and not be dependent on others. When you are dependent on someone (as when you were a child), you give up your power to that person (as a child has no power) and allow that person to take over your life.

But there is a difference between reaching out for help, and expecting to be rescued from your pain, your dependence, or your feelings of helplessness. Start looking to yourself for answers. Reach out to others, but remember that caring for yourself is ultimately up to you. Ask others for support, but don't expect them to rescue you. And most important, remember that if you can take care of yourself, you will be able to move beyond victimization.

LEARN TO SAY NO!

Another aspect of learning to take care of yourself is learning to say no. Do you believe you have a *right* to say no? Learning to say no is very difficult for those who have been victimized. As a child, if you had said no to the abuser, you may very well have been punished or abused even more severely. Generally speaking, saying no is not something we were given permission to do as children.

Now you must give *yourself* permission. Start by practicing saying no whenever you are alone in your house or car. Say it softly at first, until you can shout it out. Start saying no to people who want something from you, beginning with the least threatening person. For example, you may want to start by saying no to telephone solicitors. Instead of listening patiently while they drone on and on, politely say, "No, thank you, I'm not interested," right away.

Linda would practice saying no even when she didn't necessarily feel that strongly about the situation. Finally, she was ready to tackle the big challenge of saying no to someone who needed her. She remembered how many times she had needed someone when she was a child and how often no one helped. But Linda learned that she couldn't change her past by rescuing others. The more she learned to take care of her own needs, the less she needed to rescue others. She also learned that others can and will take care of themselves and that by rescuing her friends so often, she was actually enabling them to continue being victims themselves.

Learning to say no is basic to getting rid of a victim mentality. If you have not taken an assertiveness-training class, by all means do so (most community colleges offer courses). It will help you to learn your rights as a human being and will give you practice in standing up for yourself. If there are no such classes in your area, read the book *Your Perfect Right,* by Robert Alberti and Michael Emmons, or *When I Say No,*

I Feel Guilty by Manuel J. Smith. These books are invaluable to your becoming assertive rather than aggressive and to your learning constructive ways of communicating your desires in a way that people can understand.

Practice saying no to your loved ones, to your friends, to salespeople, and to those who want a favor. Learn that you can be loved even if you don't always do their bidding. Learn how good it feels to take care of your needs first. Feel the power that comes from asserting your needs and feelings.

Getting Comfortable Saying No

1. Complete the following sentences to better understand your fears about saying no:

   When I say no I . . .
   When I say no I . . .
   When I say no I feel . . .
   When I say no I feel . . .

   Examples

   When I say no I sound like my father.
   When I say no I feel afraid people will get angry with me.
2. Put up a giant poster or some sort of sign with "No!" on it. Place it somewhere prominent.
3. Repeat the following affirmation over and over to yourself: *It is okay to say no.*
4. Complete the following sentence several ways: When I say no I feel better about myself because . . .
5. Practice saying no often. Say it out loud when you are alone. Say no in front of the mirror. Use different intonations. This will make it easy to say it when you need to. Practice so that it feels natural when you use it.
6. Think of five situations in which you would like to say

no. (For instance, when a fellow employee asks for a ride to work and you'd rather drive alone, or when someone wants to go to a movie you don't wish to see.) List them in order of difficulty. On a weekly basis, begin saying no to the less difficult situations and work your way up to the most difficult.

YOUR CHOICES AND RIGHTS

One thing that you have now that you lacked as a child is real choice. As a child you were bound to your environment. You could not change your parents, and you could not leave your parental home. But now, if you do not like what is happening in a particular situation or relationship, you can leave. As a child you did not have a choice; as an adult you do. It is important to remember that.

Victims believe they have no choices. They feel that all decisions are made for them, that they have to go along with others' decisions and desires. When you were a child, you were a victim of sexual abuse because you virtually had no control over your life. Adults controlled you and dictated your behavior. Your parents expected you to behave according to *their* rules. If you broke those rules you were punished, ignored, or in some way made to know that you were being bad. If you wanted to be loved, accepted, or not punished, you obeyed the rules.

Now, as an adult, you may still believe that you must obey other people's rules in order to be accepted or to avoid punishment. This keeps you in the role of child or victim. Break a few rules! Choose to follow the rules *you* believe in and not follow those you do not! Better yet, make up some of your own rules!

Your Right to Your Body

When you were a child, it seemed as if everyone (especially adults) had easy access to you. Whenever the abuser wanted to have access to your body, he just reached out and grabbed. Whenever your parents wanted to, they could hit, push, or grab you. Now as an adult you may still behave as if you have no rights over your own body. You may allow others to abuse you by touching you when you do not want to be touched. Do not continue allowing others easy access to you. Instead, establish your boundaries. We all need to have a private psychological "space" that belongs to us and us alone. This space is both physical and emotional. We each have a "comfort zone," a given space between ourselves and others that enables us to feel safe and unthreatened.

You have the right to choose who can touch you and who can't, where you wish to be touched, for how long, and what type of touch is acceptable to you. This does not refer only to sexual touching. If you do not like your boss putting his arm around you while he is talking to you, for example, you have the right to say something about it. Be diplomatic: you could say, "I'd appreciate it if you didn't do that. It makes me feel rather awkward." If he continues to do it, you have the right to be firm. *No one,* under *any* circumstances, has the right to touch you if you do not want to be touched! This includes doctors and nurses. If their touch is bothering you, ask them to do it differently.

Your Bill of Rights

As a child, the message from your parents and from the perpetrator was that you did not have any rights. This message is *untrue.* You do count. You are important. You do have rights.

Discovering your rights and asserting yourself to get them

is an essential part of recovery. I have created a Bill of Rights for Survivors of Childhood Sexual Abuse. You can work with this one or use it as a basis for creating your own.

First, read through the following list. Then go back and mark each item that you need to incorporate into your life. Ask yourself, Why haven't I felt I've had the right to ______? What am I afraid will happen if I assume this right? Visualize yourself having this right and notice how you feel.

Bill of Rights

1. I have the right to direct the course of my own life, based on what I feel is right for me, regardless of what others feel I should do. This includes the right to decide what course of action I take to recover (therapy, support groups, assertiveness training, anger release, and so on).
2. I have a right to remember, discover, and tell the truth about the abuse and the abuser, about my parents and family of origin.
3. I have a right to be believed.
4. I have a right to all my feelings (anger, fear, pain, love, joy) and a right to express these feelings.
5. I have a right to confront those who were and are abusive, neglectful, and hurtful to me.
6. I have a right to break free from the negative behavior patterns of my family of origin and to break the cycle of abuse.
7. I have a right to choose the people I will relate to and relate to them in a manner of my choice (emotional or nonemotional, sexual or nonsexual, friendly or impersonal).
8. I have the right to say no!
9. I have the right to leave the company of any family

member or anyone else, temporarily or permanently, who either deliberately or inadvertently fails to respect me as a person or treats me in any way that I don't like.

10. I have the right to decide who touches my body, when, where, and for how long. I have the right to object to any touch.
11. I have the right to privacy and personal space.
12. I have the right to trust my feelings, perceptions, judgment, intuition, and inner experience.
13. I have the right to loving, nonsexual, nonabusive relationships with friends, parents, and children.
14. I have the right to a healthy, loving, sexually exciting, nonabusive relationship with a person I choose as a lover.
15. I have a right to have healthy, happy children who are safe from abuse.
16. I have a right to choose a life-style, including a sexual life-style, that is comfortable for me.
17. I have a right to happiness, love, health, and peace, regardless of the past.
18. I have the right to refuse to accept responsibility or blame for the actions and decisions of anyone except myself.
19. I have the right to decide whether or not I choose to work toward forgiving anyone. This includes the right of never forgiving anyone or never telling anyone of any forgiveness.
20. I have the right to develop myself as a whole person, emotionally, mentally, physically, psychologically, and spiritually.

These are your rights. Claiming them is your birthright. Standing up for them is crucial to your recovery!

VALUE YOURSELF

It is almost inevitable that abused and neglected children do not grow up *valuing* themselves. They feel inadequate, "less than," unimportant, unnecessary, and unworthy. Sexually abused children often come from families that do not see them as precious and important. How can children feel they are of value in families that do not protect them? How can children feel valuable when they are not the focus of loving attention by their family? And most important, how can children feel they are of any value if they are not taught to value *themselves?* Sexual abuse causes a child to feel devalued. If you are used by others and then tossed aside, your own needs unrecognized, what value could you possibly believe you have, aside from being an object? Because they were not valued, those who were sexually abused as children continue to neglect themselves just as they were neglected as children, and continue to *devalue* themselves as they were devalued as children.

As a recovering adult, you need to learn how to value, nurture, and love yourself, as well as to be around people who also value you. This nurturing environment will help you to build up a positive image of yourself and will increase your self-esteem. Valuing yourself includes valuing your time, your energy, your body, and your *worth.* You deserve to be treated well by others and by yourself. Surround yourself with those who are supportive of you, and begin to "weed out" those who are unsupportive, unloving, or overly critical.

Because many of your needs were not met and because of the damage to your self-image, you probably also have very little self-confidence. Without a healthy image of yourself, you will not be motivated to practice healthier attitudes and behaviors. For this reason, you will need to begin to become your own nurturing parent and give to yourself the care and support you missed as a child. What should you, as a nurturing parent, do to raise your inner child's self-esteem?

1. *Praise and compliment yourself (your inner child).* The regular use of self-praise builds self-confidence and validates your real worth. Talk to yourself lovingly, approvingly, acceptingly, reassuringly. Use affirmations frequently throughout the day.
2. *Support yourself.* Use statements like "Hey, look how well you handled that!" or "I believe in you, I know you can do it." Not only is it important for you to say it to yourself, it is important to really hear it and *take it in.* Giving yourself approval isn't enough; you must *absorb it.*
3. *Give yourself credit for your accomplishments—no matter how "insignificant" you may feel they are.* Whenever you have a success, you should praise yourself. Say out loud, "I knew I could do it!"
4. *Encourage yourself when you are troubled, sad, and afraid.* As you face your aloneness and begin to discover yourself, you will often feel afraid, angry, or sad. Your inner child may be afraid of such strong emotions. Reassure her that it is never harmful to feel our true feelings and that you will be there for comfort. Tell her it is okay to feel afraid or alone, that these feelings will pass.
5. *Tell your inner child that you will protect her.* Lying in a comfortable position, imagine you are holding your inner child. You can hold your stuffed animal or a pillow if you wish. Start saying, first in your imagination and then out loud, "I will protect you. I will never allow any harm to come to you. I will never allow anyone to abuse you or humiliate you." Say it over and over, until

your inner child hears you. Repeat this exercise at least once a week.

6. *Make certain that you get proper food, rest, and exercise.* An obvious part of self-nurturing involves taking care of yourself physically. Most sexual-abuse survivors are tremendously disrespectful of their bodies' needs. They tend to load their bodies with unhealthy food, drive them relentlessly, and refuse them adequate rest and tension-releasing exercise. Reassure your inner child: "I am going to make certain I feed you properly, that you get plenty of rest and exercise. I love you and want you to be healthy."

Nurturing Your Body

You can reeducate yourself to the importance of taking care of your body. It will be difficult, since you are probably not very in touch with your bodily needs. Start listening to your body. It will tell you what it needs. The following exercises can help you make a stronger connection with your body.

1. Complete the following sentence as many times as necessary until you have a better connection with how your body feels and what it is trying to tell you: I am your body and I feel . . . Do this exercise at least once a week.
2. Addressing each part of your body separately, complete the following sentence: I am your . . . and I feel . . .

   Examples

   I am your arm and I feel angry. I want to hit out! I want to push away the abuser! Let me hit and push!

   I am your heart and I feel sad. I feel broken and wounded.

> I need you to help me mend. Give me some comforting and nurturing. Stop eating such fatty foods. It makes it hard for me to work.

Self-care is an ongoing process. We can always learn to be more loving, nurturing, and supportive of ourselves—just as we can learn to become more loving toward others.

STEP 7

Forgiving Yourself

VICTIMS OF CHILDHOOD sexual abuse feel a tremendous amount of guilt: for the abuse itself, for things they did as a child as a result of the abuse, and for things they have done as an adult to hurt themselves and others. Recovery depends on freeing yourself from that guilt, acknowledging what you are responsible for and what you are not.

You may not be aware of your guilt. Unconscious guilt can cause you to be self-destructive, abusing your body with food, alcohol, drugs, cigarettes, self-mutilation, by being accident-prone, by sabotaging your success, or by eliciting punishment from others. This unconscious guilt may cause you to tenaciously hold onto your problems and your pain because it gives you the punishment you feel you deserve. You may have spent your life punishing yourself with one bad marriage after another, one illness after another. In her book *Necessary Losses,* Judith Viorst wrote that you may be "sentencing yourself to a lifetime of penance for a crime you didn't commit."

If you don't forgive yourself, you may continue to bring

people into your life who will punish you. You might have one negative relationship after another, never quite understanding why.

Even though you "know" from an intellectual, logical viewpoint that it wasn't your fault, you may not have forgiven yourself for your involvement in the abuse (for being submissive or passive, for not telling anyone, for your body's response).

You cannot be held responsible for any so-called choices you made concerning the sexual abuse, because you could not make a *free* choice. A free choice is made when you understand the consequences of your actions and when you are not coerced, bribed, intimidated, or threatened into satisfying someone else. You were only a child and incapable of making such a decision. Even if you were a teenager when the abuse occurred, you were still too young to be having sex with an adult.

It will be easier to stop blaming yourself if you can stay in touch with how innocent your inner child really was. Forgive your inner child for:

not saying no.
wanting to be loved so badly she let the abuser touch her.
protecting the abuser by not telling.
pretending she liked it.
thinking that this touch was better than no touch at all.
learning early on that she might as well get something out of it—candy, money, a trip to the carnival.

THE GUILT OF THE INNOCENT

Sometimes sexual-abuse victims try to avoid feeling their helplessness and powerlessness by blaming themselves. As a child and as a victim, you were powerless to change the situation. But it may have felt just too frightening to allow yourself to feel this powerlessness. You may have preferred instead to feel guilty, since at least then you had the *illusion* of control over what was happening to you. As Robin explained, "While my stepfather was molesting me I would just lie there. Afterward I would feel tremendously guilty. I would chastise myself for not having fought back—for just taking it. Now, I understand that I was too afraid and too powerless to fight back, but at the time all I could feel was guilt." You could also choose to feel guilty rather than to admit the truth about what really happened. It may feel less painful to blame yourself for the abuse than to face the fact that someone you love could have hurt you in such a horrible way.

Guilt can also be caused by the withholding of anger that should have (but could not have) been directed toward parents, the perpetrator, and others. Victims often direct their anger against themselves in the form of guilt. Other victims feel so guilty, ugly, and dirty inside that they believe they were and are being punished by God for being "bad"—that they "deserved" it.

It is important to distinguish between *neurotic* guilt and *real* guilt. Neurotic guilt is misplaced guilt, when you have done nothing to feel guilty about. When you feel guilty rather than accepting your helplessness as a child, for instance, that is neurotic guilt. If you continue to believe that God caused the abuse in order to punish you for being a bad child, that is also clutching onto neurotic guilt.

Real guilt, on the other hand, is a necessary social emotion. It is our conscience's way of preventing us from doing things we will later regret. Our society would fall apart if we were incapable of feeling real guilt. Real guilt is felt when we have violated our own moral code, gone against our own value and belief systems. If you do something of your own volition, without coercion or intimidation, that you know is morally wrong, then you will suffer real, healthy guilt. The purpose of this guilt is to discourage you from doing it again. But if you were coerced and intimidated into submitting to something that was harmful to you, you did not make a free choice. Your guilt cannot be real, no matter how real it seems.

Forgive Yourself

1. List everything you feel guilty about concerning the sexual abuse.

   Examples

   I feel guilty for not saying no.
   I feel guilty for not telling.
2. For each thing you have listed, give at least three reasons why you now believe you did it.

   Examples

   I didn't say no because I was afraid to.
   I didn't say no because I wanted his attention.
   I didn't say no because I didn't really understand what he was doing.
3. Complete the following sentence for *each* item on your list:
   I am not responsible for . . .

   Examples

   I am not responsible for not saying no.
   I am not responsible for not telling.
4. Complete the following sentence for *each* thing on your list:
   I forgive myself for . . .

   Examples

   I forgive myself for not saying no.
   I forgive myself for not telling.

Part of forgiving yourself requires that you also forgive your body for responding and for any pleasure it may have felt during the abuse. Your body may have responded to the touching, no matter how much your *mind* fought it or felt repulsed by it. Some victims have experienced orgasms even though they were being traumatized, hated the perpetrator, or were terrified. This betrayal by your own body is sometimes the hardest to forgive. A child does not know that her body can respond without her consent, or even that it can respond in such a way at all. You may have felt that you must have wanted the sexual act, otherwise why would your body feel pleasure? In addition, the perpetrator may have used the fact that your body was responding to manipulate you into believing that you really wanted it.

Now it is time to forgive your body for participating. It is especially important to forgive the parts of your body that were directly involved in the sexual acts, the parts of your body that felt any pleasure. Forgive your hands for touching his penis, forgive your breasts for responding to his touch, forgive your genitals for being stimulated.

Some victims still feel heat or pain in their hands from being forced to touch a penis. Many women still hate their breasts or their genitals because the abuser touched them. Just as you were innocent, your body was innocent as well. Stop punishing and hating your body for doing what it was made to do—react to stimuli, respond to touch, give you pleasure when touched. Stop hating it when it is a perfectly good and normal body. Your body did not betray you. It was tricked, just as you were.

Forgive Your Body

1. Lie down in a comfortable position on your back with your eyes closed. Take a few deep breaths and then start to breath normally. Try to relax your body as much as

possible. Tighten the muscles of your toes and feet and hold this tension as long as you can, breathing all the while. Then relax the muscles. Say, "I forgive you, toes and feet." Repeat tightening, relaxing, and forgiving each part of your body. There may be parts of your body that you don't feel you need to forgive, but do so anyway. Make certain that you particularly include your genitals, breasts, hands, and mouth. You may have a difficult time forgiving certain parts of your body, but continue repeating "I forgive you" until you feel it. When you have finished, take some deep breaths and imagine that a cleansing, refreshing breeze is going through your entire body, bringing healing and forgiveness. Relax a few minutes and pay attention to your feelings about your body before getting up. Write down your reactions in your journal.

2. For each part of your body that you feel betrayed you, complete the following sentence: I forgive you,______, for______.

   Examples

   I forgive you, arm, for not pushing him away.

   I forgive you, vagina, for feeling some pleasure.

3. Self-healing rituals can bring a sense of being reborn, cleansed, and refreshed. Soak yourself in a hot bath or Jacuzzi. Imagine that all the residues of the abuse are being soaked *out* of you through your skin. Visualize the impurities flowing out of your genitals, breasts, lips, mouth, anus—any place that was "contaminated" by the abuser. Now imagine loving energy pouring *into* your body. Visualize yourself being reborn into a pure body that will keep its integrity throughout your lifetime. Emerge cleansed, inside and out.

FORGIVING YOURSELF FOR WHAT YOU DID AS A CHILD

You also need to forgive yourself for things you did in childhood as a consequence of being hurt by the abuse. You may have become very angry and disturbed, acting out your anger and pain by hurting or abusing yourself, others, or your pets. Unable to express your anger toward the perpetrator, you may have vented your anger at those who were smaller and weaker than yourself. Since you hated yourself for being weak and helpless, you hated others who were weak as well. This behavior may have begun in childhood and continued into adulthood.

As a child who was introduced to sex too early, you may have initiated sex play with other children, perhaps through dolls, in an attempt to deal with the reality you experienced. It is also common for victims to have sexual feelings toward other children. As Fran confessed, "I remember feeling appalled at myself one time when I was baby-sitting a little toddler. I was twelve, and it was right after I had been molested. While I was changing his diapers I was suddenly overwhelmed with the desire to suck his penis. I felt sexually excited and angry at the same time. I wanted to hurt him like I had been hurt. I felt so afraid and disgusted with myself."

Memories like these can make you feel horrible about yourself. You suddenly feel no better than the perpetrator. There are several things to remember so that you can begin to forgive yourself:

1. You were a confused, disturbed child or adolescent who was acting out your pain.
2. You had been sexualized too early, before you were emotionally and physically equipped to handle it.
3. You had not developed a moral code, which is true of all children.
4. You are different from the perpetrator because you are

trying to change so that you won't hurt anyone like that again.

Just as you are not *bad* because of what someone else did to you (the sexual abuse), you are also not *bad* because of any sexual and cruel acts you committed *as a child* as a consequence of the abuse you sustained. You may feel you are responsible for these actions, but in fact you are no more responsible for them than for the sexual abuse you endured. Try to be forgiving of yourself for being a disturbed child.

Forgive Yourself for Childhood Actions

1. List all the things you did as a child as a result of the abuse.

   Examples

   I feel guilty about sexually touching my little brother.

   I feel guilty about being so cruel to my dog.
2. For each thing you have listed, write at least three reasons why you now believe you did it.

   Examples

   I touched my brother because I had been sexualized too early.

   I touched my brother because I was angry at males.

   I touched my brother because he was weaker than me and it made me feel powerful.
3. Complete the following sentence for each listing under #1:

   I was not responsible for . . .

   Examples

   I was not responsible for touching my brother.

4. Complete the following sentence for each listing under #1:

   I forgive myself for . . .

   Examples

   I forgive myself for touching my brother.

If you still believe you were old enough to be held accountable for your actions (under sixteen is *probably* not old enough), and if you believe you acted freely and on your own accord, you may be suffering from real, healthy guilt. While real guilt can serve a positive function in our society, holding onto your guilt feelings does *not* serve a positive function. If you have decided that you indeed feel real guilt about something, it will be important to remember the following:

1. Learn from your actions so that you do not repeat them. Why was it a mistake to do this? Did you hurt someone else? What were some of the other consequences? If you have learned from your mistake, and you do not wish to repeat it, then you no longer need to feel guilty about it. Let it go.
2. You will now need to find some way to atone for what you have done, before you rid yourself of your guilt. It is important to be *accountable* for your actions and behavior. Being accountable can take various forms:

- Admitting your transgression to yourself and the person or persons you hurt.
- Apologizing to the persons you hurt.
- Making amends or restitution.

FORGIVING YOURSELF FOR YOUR ACTIONS AS AN ADULT

Once you are able to forgive yourself for the abuse and for your actions as a consequence of the abuse, you will also be able to forgive yourself for the ways you learned to cope with your pain as an adult. There are two methods in which you acted out your disturbance: (1) acts against yourself and (2) acts against others.

In dealing with the first method, you must forgive yourself for being promiscuous, for being a prostitute, working in a massage parlor, or any other "deviant" sexual activities you were involved with. You were just doing what you had been taught to do—to trade your body for attention, favors, or money. Forgive yourself for all the other ways you punished yourself or learned to cope, including compulsive behaviors such as gambling, overeating, or lying. Don't hold your past against yourself. Forgive yourself.

For acts against others, remember that you *are* responsible for the things you have done *as an adult,* even though they too may have been a consequence of the abuse you sustained. You may have taken your anger out on your children, other children, or pets. You may have sexually abused a child, stolen money from someone, physically or emotionally abused your mate. You will need to make amends to those you have hurt before you can be relieved of your guilt and be able to forgive yourself. Learn from your mistake. Get therapy if you need it to stop hurting others. Make a commitment to yourself to never hurt someone like that again. Admit to the person you hurt that what you did was wrong, apologize, and make restitution to this person in the best way possible. If the person you hurt needs therapy as a result of your actions, you should offer to pay for it.

Forgive Yourself for Actions Against Others

You should now be ready to forgive yourself.

1. Make a list of all the things you have done as an adult that you feel real guilt about, those things you genuinely feel you were responsible for, that you feel you had some choice about. Include all those things that involved hurting another person ("I physically abused my daughter") or had a consequence to another person ("I lost all my husband's money gambling").

   Examples

   I feel guilty for not protecting my own children better.

   I feel guilty for stealing money from my company.
2. For each thing you have listed, write at least three reasons why you now believe you did it.

   Examples

   I didn't protect my children because I had blocked out my own abuse.

   I didn't protect my children because I wasn't protected as a child.

   I didn't protect my children because I didn't want to lose their father.
3. Complete the following sentence for *each* thing that is on your list:

   I *am* responsible for . . .

   Example

   I *am* responsible for not protecting my children.
4. Complete the following sentence for *each* thing on your list:

   I forgive myself for . . .

Example

I forgive myself for not protecting my children.

All people make mistakes as part of being human. You don't need to continue to be critical of yourself, to suffer or punish yourself. You do need to learn from your mistakes, to be accountable for your behavior, and to forgive yourself.

Forgiving yourself is different from forgiving the perpetrator or your parents. You may never be able to forgive the abuser or your family for victimizing you as a child, nor are you required to in order to recover. But recovery *does* depend on you forgiving *yourself.* Self-forgiveness is not optional, it is essential. It is an act of humanity, self-care, and self-love.

CONCLUSION

Recovery: What It Is and What It's Not

AT THIS POINT in your recovery process, stop and give yourself credit for what you have accomplished so far. Your recovery really began when you first addressed the issue of your sexual abuse. If you then made a commitment to recover, if you faced the truth about your abuse, if you have begun to release your anger, and if you started resolving your relationship with your parents, you have already completed much of the *work*. Now it will be a matter of picking up the pieces of your life and starting over again, learning new ways of relating to others, and, most important, taking care of yourself, healing yourself, and loving yourself.

Yet sometimes we look so far ahead that we don't see the accomplishments we have already made. We attempt to reach such difficult goals that we don't give ourselves credit for all the smaller changes we have made along the way. Recovery results from an accumulation of small transformations, rather than one great, sudden change. Small changes can add up to big changes if we nurture them along the way.

RECOGNIZING YOUR CHANGES

In what ways have you *already* recovered? When you made your commitment to recovery, you listed a number of reasons *why you wanted to recover.* Return to this list to see how many of these changes you have already made.

Another way of recognizing your changes is to make a list of all the ways you have recovered so far. Be sure to include all your positive changes, both big and small. Save your list and add to it whenever you observe another change. Keep your list where you can see it often. In compiling your list, be sure you answer these questions:

In what ways is my life different today than it was when I started the recovery process?
How am I different?
What new or different feelings am I experiencing?
What new insights have I had?
What changes have supportive people noticed?

It may help you with your list if you go back to the list of long-term effects of sexual abuse in the first chapter of this book. Look at the symptoms you checked off when you first started reading this book. How many of these symptoms do you still have? Remind yourself of all the work it has taken for you to have reached this point.

If you feel stuck and cannot think of too many ways in which you have recovered, ask those in your group, close friends, or supportive family members what changes they have noticed. Others often notice our changes before we do.

Doreen was unable to notice the changes occurring in her recovery program. She had been in individual therapy with me for two years and in one of my support groups for a year and a half. When she had first come to see me she had been completely unable to articulate her feelings. She would also become very confused when others in the group spoke to her. Trying to communicate with Doreen could be taxing at times for everyone concerned. But she had made incredible progress. Now it was a pleasure to talk to her. She expressed herself well and understood what others were saying right away without having to question and clarify. Nevertheless, in spite of this tremendous growth, Doreen was becoming discouraged because she was still experiencing occasional depression.

One night we went around the room giving each woman a chance to tell the group what changes she saw in herself, and when we came to Doreen, she drew a blank. "I don't think I have changed at all. All the rest of you are really improving your lives, but my life is just the same as when I started." I asked the other group members if they had noticed any changes in Doreen. Nearly everyone told her how they had seen her change. Much of the feedback centered around the issue of how much easier it was to be around her now. Doreen heard how amazed they were with her changes and how sad they were for her that she had not noticed. This was greatly comforting. She realized that one reason her changes were less noticeable to her was because they involved how she related to other people.

If you are afraid to ask others whether they see changes in you, go back to photographs of yourself before you started the recovery process. Many of my clients have been struck by how much they have *physically* changed during the time they have been working on the abuse issues. In addition, read your old journal entries. These will all remind you of how much better you are now!

During her first six months of recovery, Joan noticed several changes in herself. She made the following list:

1. I can talk about the sexual abuse I suffered a lot more easily.

2. I speak up for myself instead of letting others walk all over me so much.
3. I am more aware of my body.
4. I express my emotions more.
5. I look more relaxed.

Sylvia's list, after two years:

1. I am able to express my anger now.
2. I don't have headaches anymore.
3. I don't hit my son anymore.
4. I quit that job I hated.
5. I can now have sex with a man.
6. I trust people more.

Terri's list, after three years:

1. I no longer see everything as black and white, as all or nothing.
2. I take time for myself now: I feel my own separate identity.
3. I have separated from my mother.
4. I can have an honest, nonabusive, equal relationship with others. I don't lie to others anymore, I don't let myself be abused anymore, and I have relationships with people who can give to me as much as I give to them.

My own list, after five years:

1. I am more patient with others and myself, less critical and judgmental.
2. I have *much* better relationships and have improved my communication skills.
3. I do not allow my mother to abuse me any longer.

4. I am taking better care of myself in every way—physically, emotionally, and spiritually.
5. I am no longer a victim or a martyr.

YOUR MOST SUBTLE ENEMY: RESISTANCE

While you certainly want to achieve recovery and all its benefits, there may also be a part of you that will *resist* these changes and resist recovery. Sometimes change is just too frightening to us. Even positive change can cause us to feel shaky, off-balance, off-center. At other times, we resist a particular change because of a conflict inside us, because of actually wanting two things at once.

Many clients, for example, experience a conflict between wanting to feel their emotions and not wanting to. We all tend to fear losing control. Even those who have learned all the benefits of expressing feelings sometimes resist it from time to time, out of habit or fear. Since allowing yourself to feel and express your emotions is such a necessary and vital part of recovery, you may need to address your conflict about feeling or not feeling your emotions from time to time. To examine your ambivalence in any conflict, write down both sides of your inner argument until you feel complete.

I want to feel my feelings because . . .
I don't want to feel my feelings because . . .

Try this exercise whenever you have a conflict between wanting one thing and wanting something else that is the opposite or is seemingly incompatible. Continue completing the sentences until you feel finished, alternating each time between your two desires. For instance:

I want marriage because I don't want to be alone.

I want solitude because I need my time alone.
I want marriage because I love children.
I want solitude because I need peace and quiet.
I want marriage because I feel I have something to give.
I want solitude because sometimes I feel that I only hurt others.

Some clients resist getting better because they are afraid of what life will be like when they are recovered. As Hope confessed to me, "It feels scary to think about recovering. I won't be coming to the group any longer, and I won't see you. I don't think I want to give it all up—the support, the caring. I don't really have any friends." Anita shared her fear of recovery from a different perspective: "I am beginning to realize that from this point on *I* am responsible for any decisions I now make. I can no longer blame anyone else for my current choices. I've been blaming my parents for my past choices, but now I have to be an adult and make certain that I can live with my decisions. It's really frightening."

Sabotaging any progress is another way of resisting recovery. Some survivors cannot really trust it when they experience success or happiness because they are afraid these new good times will not continue. When they finally achieve their goals (a new job, a healthy relationship), some survivors become afraid they won't be able to "keep it up" or continue to perform at a high rate. Because of these fears, they set themselves up for failure. Out of fear they sometimes deliberately create problems in their own lives, risking something dangerous or unhealthy to sabotage their recovery. They sabotage their own happiness or success as a way of feeling they have some measure of control over their lives—so they won't have to worry about "the worst" happening, or someone else taking what's good away from them.

Other survivors have different reasons for sabotaging any progress toward their recovery:

- They still have a need to punish their parents or the perpetrator ("I don't want them to see me happy; I want them to know they destroyed my entire life.")
- They fear success ("I know what failure feels like, but success seems scary.")
- They want to remain invisible ("If I am successful, people will notice me.")
- They are afraid they will be abusive with their power like their parents were.

As you can see, the common thread that runs through all these reasons for self-sabotage is fear. If you identify with any of the above reasons for self-sabotage, you need to face this fear. Oftentimes survivors do not know when they are sabotaging their recovery. Below are some common examples of self-sabotaging behavior:

- Suddenly finding fault in your lover or mate, especially when the relationship had been going well.
- Finding fault in a job you have previously been happy with, dropping out of school, stopping your exercise or diet program or any other self-improvement regimen.
- Ending therapy too soon.

Whenever you feel "stuck," when you suspect you may be resisting or sabotaging your recovery, ask yourself, "What steps do I need to still work on?" and go back to that step. Reread the chapter, follow the recommendations, complete the exercises, and read other books on the subject (see the Recommended Reading list at the end of this book). Also, ask yourself, "What else do I need to do in order to recover?" There may be other steps you need to take that are not in this book. You have these answers inside of you.

BE REALISTIC

It is unrealistic to expect recovery to remove all pain and anger regarding your sexual abuse. The hurt was so deep that it will resurface periodically; the anger was so intense that it will re-erupt from time to time. You can't change the past, but you certainly can *react* to it differently.

Recovery from sexual abuse does not mean that all pain will stop. Some people will continue to hurt and disappoint you, and life will continue to present its share of problems and disappointments—as is the case for every other human being. Now, however, you are better equipped to respond to life's ups and downs, better able to bounce back after a crisis. Instead of being so weighed down with the past that any current problem becomes unmanageable, you are now able to face each new problem on its own, as a separate occurrence.

Do not expect all your fears to disappear, either. Fear is a normal part of life. It's just that you will fear *life* less. Failure will be less threatening, since you have experienced so much success during your recovery program. You will especially be less afraid of other people, since you have already faced your real enemies. Having had the courage to face your abusers (literally or through your imagination), you will be more able to confront your present and future adversaries.

If you have a healthy attitude toward recovery, you will also accept the fact that all of your symptoms may not completely disappear, that some may resurface when you are under stress, or in a situation that reminds you of the abuse. Some problems will take longer to work through but will gradually subside, while others may take a lifetime to work through. A few may not go away at all, but will remain a permanent testament to the fact that you are a survivor of childhood sexual abuse.

Real change typically involves two steps forward and one step backward. One day you might feel on top of the world, full of self-respect and high self-esteem, only to have the props knocked out from under you the next day. At these times you may well feel as though you have made absolutely no progress. When this happens, remind yourself of the ways you have changed in order to counter this "all or none" conclusion.

Realize, too, that your old symptoms can be warnings that something is not right. When you sense them returning (migraine headaches, overeating, losing your temper at people at work), ask yourself, "What is going on in my life now that is similar to when I was being sexually abused? Am I involved with someone who reminds me of one of my parents or the perpetrator?"

When Lynn started a new job, many of her old symptoms immediately returned. She began having difficulty sleeping, she became very withdrawn from her friends, and her appetite disappeared. "I don't know what's wrong," she told her group. "I thought I was almost recovered. Now suddenly I feel like nothing has changed."

With some help from the group, Lynn figured out that her new boss reminded her of her stepfather, who used to rape her every night. "My God," she exclaimed, "he even talks like him! Instead of asking me to do something he just orders me to do it. It's like living with my stepfather all over again." Making this important connection between her boss and her stepfather helped Lynn to once again feel in control of her life. Knowing she wouldn't be able to work under such conditions because it made her feel like a victim again, she decided to risk confronting him. Surprisingly, her boss was receptive to her feedback. Lynn was truly recovering and was now a survivor. Even though her past symptoms had briefly returned, she did not let them defeat her. Once she realized why they were back, she was able to take steps to improve the situation.

WHAT RECOVERY WILL MEAN TO YOU

As you recover, you will begin to live life more in the present and actually experience more emotional peace of mind. You will feel a sense of freedom from much of the emotional pain associated with the past.

Recovery means freedom—freedom to make choices based on what is good for you: It means knowing who you are and what you like. It means once again being able to enjoy your body, your sensations, your relationships, and the feeling of being alive. Because you have had the courage to "stick it out" through incredibly painful times, even when the process seemed absolutely endless, you have developed an inner strength and courage—a knowledge that comes from having endured and conquered one of the most devastating experiences imaginable.

In addition, you will begin to feel like breaking out of your self-imposed isolation and will be more willing to reach out to others. This may mean seeking a one-to-one intimate relationship, making friends, or opening up more to those people already in your life. Your greater trust in yourself will make you more trusting of others. You will know what recovery feels like.

In the first section of this book, we discussed the many benefits of recovery. They haven't changed, only now they may have started becoming part of your life:

- Higher self-esteem.
- Improved relationships.
- Improved sexuality.
- Increased ability to understand, express, and release your emotions.
- Relief from your physical symptoms.
- Increased control over your life.
- Heightened awareness of yourself and your environment.
- Ability to differentiate the past from the present.

- Shedding of negative behaviors, beliefs, and defenses.
- Discovery of who you really are.
- Release of false hopes and unreasonable expectations.
- Waning of your attraction to chaos.

These positive changes do not comprise a complete listing by any means. Compose your own, personal itemizing of what recovery means to *you,* what changes you want to make in order to feel you have recovered sufficiently. Include those things you want to *let go of* (including inappropriate survival skills you no longer need, negative beliefs, and erroneous parental messages) and the things you want to be free to do and free from doing. Think of this as a list of your goals for recovery, if you wish.

I want to let go of . . .
I want to be free of . . .
I want to be free to . . .
I want to be able to . . .

As you look over your recovery list, notice how realistic or unrealistic it is. Have you listed goals that are impractical, given who you are and your present circumstances? Or is it feasible that you could reach these goals?

The following recovery list that Anita put together for herself is both specific and realistic. Her goals—well within possibility, considering who she is and how far she has already come—are hardly grandiose transformations but rather practical changes.

I know I am recovering when:
I can feel okay about doing things by myself.
I will want to have a relationship with a man.
I will be able to express my feelings as they come up.

I can feel comfortable in a setting with more than one person.
I can take in good feelings from other people.
I can give more of myself to the people I care about.
I am not so hard on myself.
I am able to be more honest with myself and other people.
I am working in a satisfying job.
I am no longer sexualizing things that aren't sexual.
I can reach out to other people.

Clients often have unreasonable expectations concerning their recovery. Make sure you do not set yourself up for disappointment and failure. Try to gain a realistic perspective of who you can become and what you are capable of accomplishing. What can you reasonably expect of yourself? What can you realistically look forward to?

The following recovery list is both too general and unrealistic:

I know I am recovering when:
I am no longer needy.
I can be a good mother.
I can feel comfortable in the world.

I am no longer needy. (Problem: Everyone is needy. There is nothing *wrong* with being needy—in fact, I encourage clients to work on being more accepting of their neediness. Perhaps this goal could be changed to "When my life is not *dictated* by my neediness, when I don't do things that are unhealthy because of my needy feelings.")

I can be a good mother. (What *is* a "good mother"? This indicates a certain unreasonable pressure to perform as a mother. Perhaps the goal could be broken down into smaller, less general tasks, such as being more patient with her children or being less demanding of them.)

I can feel comfortable in the world. (Again, a goal too broad and unrealistic. Better and more possible would be to aim to feel more comfortable with the opposite sex, or to be more comfortable speaking in front of a group. Moreover, it's important to remember that *no one* is ever totally comfortable all the time.)

People with realistic goals achieve more, since they are continually reinforced and rewarded by their successes.

OTHER ISSUES AND PROBLEMS

You will need to accept the fact that just because you have completed the recovery program in this book doesn't mean that you are not still suffering from *other* problems. Some of these problems may have come out of the sexual abuse but are now separate issues. If you are an alcohol, drug, or food abuser, you may discover that these behaviors subside as you continue the recovery process. On the other hand, these problems can also take on a life of their own and develop into a full-blown problem that needs to be dealt with separately. You may now want to seek help for these problems through the assistance of experts in the field or by joining a support group such as Overeaters Anonymous (OA), Alcoholics Anonymous (AA), Narcotics Anonymous (NA), or any of the other anonymous groups available.

Now that your mind is not fixed on the sexual abuse alone, you can focus on other growth issues. You may discover, for example, that you need to learn more parenting skills. Parents Anonymous offers help and support for those who still tend to be abusive to their children. Parent Effectiveness Training (PET) is offered at most adult schools. It teaches effective parenting skills to help gain control of yourself and your children.

Many survivors of sexual abuse continue to suffer from problems with family, relationships, and intimacy. Couples counseling or family therapy may now be in order to help you to understand your mate and children better, to help them to better understand you, and to assist the entire family in healing from the ordeal of your sexual abuse. In addition, better communication skills may be needed so that all of you can be more open, honest, and clear in your communications with one another.

Codependency

Because many survivors of childhood sexual abuse come from abusive, violent, alcoholic, or chemically dependent families, they have learned dysfunctional ways of relating to others and may have become "addicted" to the dysfunctional family system. Many have developed a *codependent* personality—one that is dependent on other people and things for a sense of self. Most counselors and other clinicians now believe that alcoholism, in particular, affects the entire family to such an extent that family members are labeled *coalcoholics* or *codependents.*

If you are married to or tend to get involved with alcoholic or other chemically dependent people, or if one or both of your parents were alcoholics, you may want to look into two groups, Al-Anon and ACA (Adult Children of Alcoholics). Both programs are sponsored by Alcoholics Anonymous to help the codependent person deal with such problems as difficulties with intimacy, exaggerated need for the approval of others, difficulty making decisions and changes, a tendency to lie and exaggerate, a tendency to look for people to take care of or to rescue, a need to control others, and an inability to be spontaneous or to have fun. If you suffer from any of these problems, you may want to consider the possibility that you are a codependent.

Sexuality and Sexual Identity

Although most sexual concerns will be alleviated through the recovery process, some survivors experience specific problems regarding their sexuality that they will now need to address. Such problems as lack of sexual desire, painful intercourse, and inability to reach orgasm may linger on. A wonderful book, *Incest and Sexuality: A Guide to Understanding and Healing,* by Wendy Maltz and Beverly Holman, can be helpful in your work on specific sexual issues. In addition, you may want to seek the help of an experienced, licensed sex therapist.

Many survivors of childhood sexual abuse suffer from sexual identity problems. During the recovery process, some women find themselves attracted to other women and start homosexual relationships for the first time in their lives. Still others are repulsed by men and fear they will never be able to have a relationship with one. Once the program is completed, however, most participants are no longer as confused about their sexual preference. Many women who were startled by their homosexual feelings discover that once they have released their anger toward the perpetrator, their heterosexual orientation is restored.

Some lesbian women, while they are working on recovery, become confused when they suddenly stop feeling attracted to their partner or to women altogether. Some lesbian clients go through a time of confusion, not being sure whether they are with women out of choice or whether it is just because they are afraid, angry, or repulsed by men due to the sexual abuse. This confusion usually does not last. Clients tend to come to a better understanding of who they are and who they choose to be with as more of the sexual abuse issues are resolved. But some women need further help. *Incest and Sexuality* also offers help for sexual-identity confusion and help for lesbian couples with their sexual problems.

MOURNING THE OLD, EMBRACING THE NEW

Moving on means letting go. Just as moving to a new house means saying good-bye to the old house and the old neighborhood, moving on emotionally requires saying good-bye to many of our old, comfortable ways and beliefs. Any good-bye is painful. You will need to set aside a time for looking back, a time for mourning. This will help you to stop resisting change and will help squelch any tendency to sabotage your progress toward recovery. Mourning the old will not stop you from feeling excited about the new. It is not uncommon to be at the threshold of change, feeling simultaneously exhilarated and sad.

You can look forward to a time when you no longer feel in constant crisis, a time when you no longer feel as if the trauma is controlling your life. The future can be faced knowing that you are in control of yourself and your own destiny. You are no longer being controlled by your past, your parents, the perpetrator, or anyone else.

Don't sell yourself short: Working through the trauma of sexual abuse is one of the most difficult tasks anyone can undertake. You have a tremendous amount of courage for getting this far in your recovery, for admitting that you were sexually abused, and for facing all the horrible truths you've encountered along the way. *Most people do not face these things.* The majority of sexually abused never admit the abuse, minimize the effects it had on them, and then continue to abuse themselves and others. You have withstood unbearable pain, more pain than any human being should ever be exposed to. Give yourself credit for being one of the brave few with the courage to begin the journey and the determination to stick it out when the pain was intolerable.

Celebrate your courage; celebrate your victories both large and small; celebrate your *freedom!* Take care of yourself, love yourself. You deserve it. Continue to allow yourself to feel and express your emotions. Through your emotions you have found a way to make changes and face problems. No matter who tells you *not* to feel (and there will be many), you now know better. You know you are on the right path.

You have a heart that is capable of being full of love. But as a child, both your innocence and your ability to love were corrupted. Now, as you become healthier, you can reclaim that ability to love and be loved. You can reclaim your right to innocence. As my client Connie put it: "My heart had a fence around it to protect it from being hurt. I think I am now ready to tear down that fence. I don't think I need it anymore."

APPENDIX

To the Mates and Loved Ones of Survivors

IF YOU CARE about someone who was a victim of childhood sexual abuse you probably want to know how you can help that person recover. And you probably have a lot of questions about what your lover/friend/sibling/parent is going through while working through the recovery program. Their behavior may puzzle, worry, frighten, or anger you. There will probably be many times when you get impatient and feel like "throwing in the towel" concerning the relationship.

One of the best ways for you to be supportive is to listen to their story and their feelings. Victims of childhood sexual abuse have had to hold in their feelings and their secret for a long time, and part of the healing process for them is to be able to freely talk about it now. Careful listening can provide you with important insights about what your loved one is going through.

You need not rescue or give advice. In fact, advice may backfire, because it may sound like disapproval. Moreover, advice that may seem sound and reasonable to you may actually be countertherapeutic to the person recovering. If, for example, the survivor is being encouraged by the therapist or group members to stay away from her family of origin for a time, it does not help if you in all your best intentions urge reconciliation and fence mending.

Carla shared her frustration about her husband's advice-giving with her support group: "All I really want my husband to do is to listen to me, but every time I try to talk to him he ends up telling me what to do, trying to solve my problems for me. I know I've learned that he is afraid of all the feelings I am expressing and that he probably just feels helpless and is trying to gain some control of the situation, but honestly, I've had it with his need to be in control!"

Most important, and a key to recovery, is that sexual-abuse victims need to know that the people closest to them are "with them," are on their side. One of the most damaging events that can occur to a survivor is to not be believed. It is vitally important that you believe it really happened, believe that the person the survivor says abused her did indeed do so. Do not minimize the extent of the trauma. It is not being made up, it is not a lie, it is not an exaggeration. If anything, survivors of childhood sexual abuse *minimize* what happened, how much it hurt them, and how terrible they feel about it.

The raw reality of childhood sexual abuse is so terrible that it is difficult to hear and sometimes difficult to believe: "When Kim told me about how her grandfather brutally raped her over and over, I just couldn't tolerate it. I had to blank it out of my mind. The visual image kept coming back, and it tormented me. I guess that's why I withdrew myself from her during that time. I wish I could have been more supportive, but I just couldn't. I even suggested to her that perhaps she was imagining it." Charlotte, my client Kim's best friend, shared this with me after Kim had told her she had to stop seeing her.

It is also vitally important that you do not blame the victim for the abuse. Implying or stating that the survivor was responsible for the sexual abuse or that the survivor must have asked for it in some way can be extremely damaging. Such statements only reinforce an already intense feeling of irrational guilt and sense of worthlessness.

Instead, you can start to understand what the survivor has endured by reading about childhood sexual abuse, talking with other survivors, and consulting with a therapist. It will help to read this entire book, but concentrate particularly on the chapters "Releasing Your Anger" and "Self-Care." This will help put in context the immense anger your loved one has and needs to release. She will be angry a great deal of the time, and if she feels comfortable releasing her anger in constructive ways around you (hitting pillows, yelling, writing anger letters) there will be less chance of her taking her anger out on you or others. The "Anger" chapter will also offer *you* constructive ways of releasing your own anger. You will need it. Frequently, victims take their anger out on those closest to them. Your mate may begin to confuse you with the perpetrator or the silent partner (the nonoffending parent), for example. If you can remember that it is not really you she is angry with, you may not react quite so volatilely yourself.

As recommended earlier, pay particular attention to the "Self-Care" chapter. It can benefit you as much as it does your loved ones. You will need to learn self-care techniques so that you do not end up putting all your needs aside and focusing only on what your loved one needs. By no means should you allow *yourself* to be used, abused, or taken advantage of. For you, self-care may mean standing up for yourself, walking away from the situation temporarily, or seeking help for yourself by joining a support group or individual therapy.

It is natural for you to tire of listening to a continuous flow of feelings. Don't expect yourself to be able to "be there" at all times. In addition, don't hold back from talking about *your* problems from time to time. But if some of your needs cannot be met right now, try to take care of them yourself or seek out friends who can help. By all means, avoid getting into an emotional place where you feel so deprived that you become demanding or abusive to the victim—the last thing needed during recovery.

Be prepared that along with feeling somewhat burned-out from listening, you may also encounter your own fear, anger, and sadness, from your own long-suppressed memories and deeply buried feelings. If you become unduly anxious, or else afraid, angry, and sad, more than empathy may be at play; you may in addition be remembering incidents of childhood sexual abuse of your own or of someone close to you.

You may also find it difficult to deal with your strong reactions toward the members of the survivor's family of origin. Sometimes partners and friends become so angry at the perpetrator or the silent partner that they can hardly bear not to unload their rage on them. While this desire is understandable, it is rarely a good idea. This would amount to "taking care" of the victim in a way that actually denies her control of the situation. The survivor needs to be the one to do the confronting, if and when it is to happen.

Some victims continue to see the perpetrator, and this is sometimes difficult for their partner to understand. Richard, the husband of my client Vicki, said in one of our sessions, "I just can't believe she wants to still see her father. He sexually molested her, for God's sake! You'd think she couldn't stand to be around him. I don't understand the hold he still has on her. Every time she sees him she is a basket case afterward, but she still insists on going over there." Richard, like many people, did not understand the strong need many victims have to try to win their parents' love, even those who have been abusive. With some education about the dynamics of childhood sexual abuse, Richard came to better understand his wife and became less critical of her. While in therapy, Richard also learned to better manage his own needs. He decided that while he no longer felt critical of his wife seeing her parents, he himself did not feel comfortable being around them. He took care of himself by telling his wife that he was no longer willing to go with her when she visited them.

The sexual relationship between survivor and partner is commonly very strained and problematic. Your partner may be unable to have sex with you for a while, or else the frequency and type of sex may be limited. Any sexual contact for the survivor is liable to become increasingly difficult: Since the trauma was sexual, it makes sense that any act of sexuality might trigger memories of the abuse. When these memories come flooding in, the survivor may not be able to distinguish you from the perpetrator, or the present from the past. As memories continue to emerge, the survivor will have clearer and clearer mental pictures of what exactly occurred, of what specific sexual acts were performed on her, of which parts of her body were touched or assaulted. This may result in particular acts or parts of her body becoming "off-limits" for a while.

Understand that the survivor's difficulties with sex stem from the abuse and are not a reflection of her feelings toward you. Knowing this, you can offer her the support she needs in order to break through the pain and distrust.

Keep in mind the reasons why a survivor has difficulty with sexuality and trust, and avoid trying to pressure her into sex with demands, guilt, or threats. If you continually push for her to meet your sexual needs, you will only set yourself up for rejection. It is essential that you not withdraw but try to keep the lines of communication open, telling her how you feel and eliciting her feelings. State your needs in as clear and nonpressuring manner as possible. Instead of saying, for example, "We haven't had sex in three weeks. How long is this going to go on?", try expressing not only your sexual needs but your desire for intimacy and closeness—something like, "I love you. Sex is important to me; it is one of the ways I can express loving feelings for you and have you express yours to me. But I don't want to pressure you into having sex unless you feel like it. Maybe we could just hold each other or give each other a massage, so that I can get some reassurance and affection and can have a way to let you know I love you."

Again, I recommend the book *Incest and Sexuality: A Guide to Understanding and Healing,* written by Wendy Maltz and Beverly Holman, as an invaluable aid in not only helping your sexual relationship with your mate but also in helping to improve your overall relationship.

Resources

CHOOSING A THERAPIST

One of the best ways of finding a competent therapist is to get a referral from someone you know. Ask another survivor, friend, co-worker, teacher, or your medical doctor. Or call your local hospital, rape-crisis helpline, or other hotline and ask them to refer you to someone who specializes in working with adults molested as children. A referral doesn't mean that this will be the therapist for you, but it usually indicates that the therapist is respected and known in the community.

Interviewing Potential Therapists

Choose your therapist carefully, taking into consideration several things: experience and training in working with survivors of childhood sexual abuse; theoretical orientation and belief system regarding sexual abuse; how he or she treats you; and, most important, *how you feel about them.* In addition, a good therapist should convey warmth, genuineness, and empathy.

The only way you are going to find out this information is to ask questions and to pay attention to how you feel in this person's presence. Answers to these relevant questions will be helpful: (1) What type of techniques do you use and what is your training in this area? (2) Do you think there is ever a situation in which a child asks for the abuse or is responsible for it? (3) Is forgiveness and family reconciliation a goal of your therapy?

While you will probably be nervous during the first few sessions and may not feel comfortable with the questions the therapist is asking, you should feel his or her respect, understanding, and support. Most assuredly, you should not feel that your experience is being minimized or that you are being judged or criticized. You should get the sense that the person really *cares* but is not a rescuer. It is not necessary that the therapist be a survivor, but if this is the case, ask how he or she reached recovery.

Many of my colleagues talk about how they can tell from the first interview whether the therapy will be productive or not, depending on how they connected with the client. Many believe it is important to have the right "fit" between client and therapist. If the therapist doesn't seem to like you or seems indifferent, you may need to keep looking. You should start the therapy process with a certain amount of warmth and connectedness between you and the therapist.

Because of the betrayal you suffered, you may have a difficult time trusting a therapist. You have the right as a client to determine what is comfortable and what is not, what you want and what you don't want. It is your legal and ethical right to not be touched without your permission.

SURVIVORS GROUPS

Survivors groups are usually facilitated by a licensed therapist or an experienced group leader who is a survivor. Some groups may charge a nominal fee. The following resources may help you find a survivors group in your area:

Alliance of Information
and Referral Services
(AIRS)
1100 W. 42nd St. Ste. 310
Indianapolis, IN 46208

Parents United
AMACU Coordinator
P.O. Box 952
San Jose, CA 95108
408/280-5055

Center for Adult Survivors
of Sexual Abuse (CASSA)
205 Avenue I, Ste. 27
Redondo Beach, CA 90277
213/379-5929

Incest Resources
Women's Center
46 Pleasant St.
Cambridge, MA 12139
617/492-1818

Looking Up
P.O. Box K
Augusta, ME 04330
207/626-3402

National Coalition Against
Sexual Assault
Austin Rape Crisis Center
P.O. Box 7156
Austin, TX 78712
512/472-8858

VOICES (Victims of Incest
Can Emerge Survivors) in
Action, Inc.
P.O. Box 148309
Chicago, IL 60614
312/327-1500

SELF-HELP GROUPS

Self-help groups do not have professional counselors and seldom have leaders. They are made up of people who have a common problem—be it incest, alcoholism, or obesity. They are generally free of charge.

The self-help groups that follow are modeled on the twelve-step program of Alcoholics Anonymous (AA). Of these groups, Incest Survivors Anonymous most pertinently addresses the subject at hand:

Incest Survivors Anony-
mous (ISA)
P.O. Box 5613
Long Beach, CA 90805-0613
213/428-5599

Adult Children of Alcoholics (ACA)
2225 Sepulveda Blvd., #200
Torrance, CA 90505
213/534-1815

Gamblers Anonymous
National Service Office
P.O. Box 17173
Los Angeles, CA 90017
213/386-8789

Narcotics Anonymous
World Service Office
16155 Wyandotte St.
Van Nuys, CA 91406
818/780-3951

Overeaters Anonymous
World Service Office
4025 Spencer St., Ste. 203
Torrance, CA 90503
213/542-8363

Sexaholics Anonymous
P.O. Box 300
Simi Valley, CA 93062

To contact one of the twelve-step groups below, consult the yellow pages of your local phone directory under "Alcoholism." You will find a number for the central office of the specific group you wish to contact. They will direct you to the nearest meeting.

Alcoholics Anonymous is recommended for survivors who are also recovering from alcoholism. AA is open to anyone who has a desire to stop drinking.

Al-Anon is targeted at the adult relatives or friends of someone who has a drinking problem.

Alateen is open to those between the ages of twelve and twenty-one who have a family member or friend with a drinking problem.

Sex and Love Addicts Anonymous is open to those who have difficulties with intimate relationships and sexuality and for those who are sexually compulsive.

The following resources are not twelve-step programs but may provide help for specific problems related to the effects of childhood sexual abuse:

Bulimia/Anorexia Self-Help
800/227-4785
in Missouri: 314/991-BASH

Cocaine Hotline (National
Institute on Drug Abuse)
800/662-HELP

Smokenders
800/323-1126
in Illinois: 312/790-3339

RECOMMENDED READING

Childhood Sexual Abuse

Angelou, Maya. *I Know Why the Caged Bird Sings.* New York: Bantam, 1980.

Armstrong, I. *Kiss Daddy Goodnight.* New York: Hawthorn, 1978.

Bass, Ellen, and Laura Davis. *The Courage to Heal: A Guide for Women Survivors of Child Sexual Abuse.* New York: Harper & Row, 1988.

Bass, Ellen, and Louise Thornton, eds. *Writings by Women Survivors of Childhood Sexual Abuse.* New York: Harper & Row, 1983.

Brady, Katherine. *Father's Days: A True Story of Incest.* New York: Dell, 1979.

Butler, Sandra. *Conspiracy of Silence: The Trauma of Incest.* San Francisco: Volcano Press, 1985.

Crewdson, John. *By Silence Betrayed: Sexual Abuse of Children in America.* Boston: Little, Brown, 1988.

Finkelhor, David. *Child Sexual Abuse: New Theory and Research.* New York: The Free Press, 1984.

Forward, Susan, and Craig Buck. *Betrayal of Innocence: Incest and Its Devastation.* Los Angeles: Jeremy P. Tarcher, 1978.

Herman, Judith. *Father-Daughter Incest.* Cambridge: Harvard University Press, 1981.

McNaran, Toni, and Yarrow Morgan, eds. *Voices in the Night: Women Speaking About Incest.* Minneapolis: Cleis Press, 1982.

Maltz, Wendy, and Beverly Holman. *Incest and Sexuality: A Guide to Understanding and Healing.* Lexington, Mass.: Lexington Books, 1987.

Masson, Jeffrey Moussaieff. *The Assault on Truth: Freud's Suppression of the Seduction Theory.* New York: Farrar Straus Giroux, 1984.

Morris, Michele. *If I Should Die Before I Wake.* New York: Dell, 1982.

Rush, Florence. *The Best-Kept Secret: Sexual Abuse of Children.* Englewood Cliffs, N.J.: Prentice-Hall, 1980.

Russell, Diana. *The Secret Trauma: Incest in the Lives of Girls and Women.* New York: Basic Books, 1986.

Child Abuse in General

Gil, Eliana. *Outgrowing the Pain: A Book for and About Adults Abused as Children.* San Francisco: Launch Press, 1983.

Miller, Alice. *Thou Shalt Not Be Aware: Society's Betrayal of the Child.* New York: New American Library, 1986.

———. *For Your Own Good: Hidden Cruelty in Child-rearing and the Roots of Violence.* New York: Farrar Straus Giroux, 1984.

———. *The Drama of the Gifted Child: The Search for the True Self.* New York: Basic Books, 1981.

Your Inner Child

Pollard, John. *Self-Parenting: The Complete Guide to Your Inner Conversations.* Malibu, Ca.: Generic Human Studies Publishing, 1987.

Whitfield, Charles. *Healing the Child Within: Discovery and Recovery for Adult Children of Dysfunctional Families.* Pompano Beach, Fla.: Health Communications, 1987.

Separating from Parents

Friday, Nancy. *My Mother/My Self.* New York: Dell Publishing, 1977.

Halpern, Howard. *Cutting Loose: An Adult Guide to Coming to Terms with Your Parents.* New York: Simon & Schuster, 1976.

Viorst, Judith. *Necessary Losses.* New York: Ballantine, 1986.

Exploring Feelings/Self-Discovery

Capacchione, Lucia. *The Creative Journal.* Chicago: Swallow Press, 1979.

Lerner, Harriet. *The Dance of Anger: A Woman's Guide to Changing the Patterns of Intimate Relationships.* New York: Harper & Row, 1986.

Lowen, Alexander. *The Betrayal of the Body.* New York: Macmillan, 1967.

———. *The Language of the Body.* New York: Macmillan, 1958.

Progoff, Ira. *At a Journal Workshop.* New York: Dialog House Library, 1975.

Assertiveness

Alberti, Robert, and Michael Emmons. *Your Perfect Right.* San Luis Obispo, Ca.: Impact, 1975.

Phelps, Stanlee, and Nancy Austin. *The Assertive Woman.* San Luis Obispo, Ca.: Impact, 1987.

Smith, Manuel J. *When I Say No, I Feel Guilty.* New York: Bantam, 1975.

Adult Children of Alcoholics

Black, Claudia. *Repeat After Me.* Denver: M.A.C. Printing, 1985.

———. *It Will Never Happen to Me!* Denver: M.A.C. Printing, 1982.

Gravitz, Herbert, and Julie Bowden. *Guide to Recovery: A Book for Adult Children of Alcoholics.* Holmes Beach, Fla.: Learning Publications, Inc., 1985.

Woititz, Janet Geringer. *Struggle for Intimacy.* Pompano Beach, Fla.: Health Communications, 1985.

———. *Adult Children of Alcoholics.* Pompano Beach, Fla.: Health Communications, 1983.

Codependency

Norwood, Robin. *Women Who Love Too Much.* Los Angeles: Jeremy P. Tarcher, 1985.

Wegscheider-Cruse, Sharon. *Choice-Making: For Co-dependents, Adult Children, and Spirituality Seekers.* Pompano Beach, Fla.: Health Communications, 1985.

Compulsive Overeating

Orbach, Susie. *Fat Is a Feminist Issue.* London: Paddington Press, 1978.

Roth, Geneen. *Feeding the Hungry Heart.* New York: Bobbs-Merrill, 1982.

Relationships

Paul, Jordan, and Margaret Paul. *Do I Have to Give Up Me to Be Loved by You?* Minneapolis: CompCare Publishers, 1983.

Peele, Stanton. *Love and Addiction.* New York: New American Library, 1975.

Drama-Seeking

Davidson, Joy. *The Agony of It All: The Drive for Drama and Excitement in Women's Lives.* Los Angeles: Jeremy P. Tarcher, 1988.

ABOUT THE AUTHOR

BEVERLY ENGEL, a licensed marriage, family, and child counselor, is a leading expert in the treatment of adults who were sexually abused as children. She is founder and director of the Center for Adult Survivors of Sexual Abuse (CASSA). She has trained hundreds of psychotherapists in how to work with survivors of sexual abuse and has conducted workshops for the Association for Humanistic Psychology and the National Organization for Women. She maintains a private practice in Southern California.